THE VISUAL DICTIONARY *of*
DINOSAURS

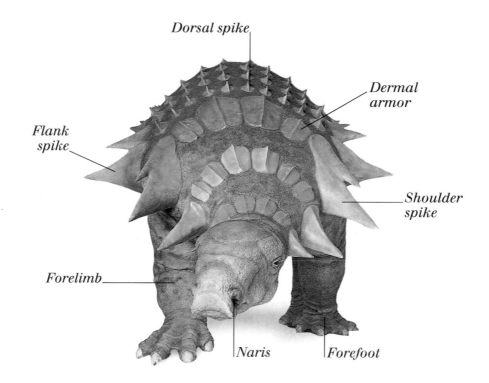

Dorsal spike

Dermal armor

Flank spike

Shoulder spike

Forelimb

Naris

Forefoot

**EXTERNAL FEATURES
OF EDMONTONIA**

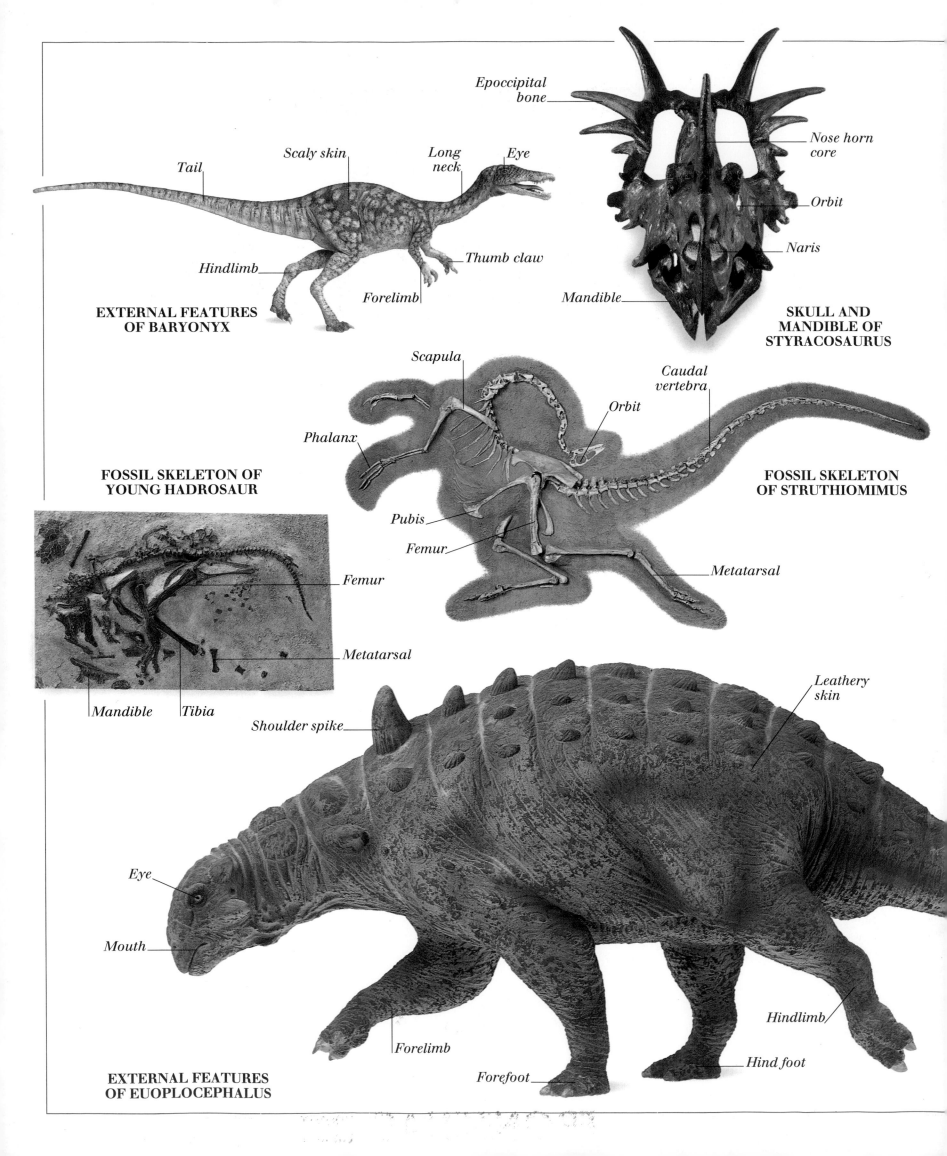

**EXTERNAL FEATURES
OF BARYONYX**

Tail

Scaly skin

Long neck

Eye

Hindlimb

Thumb claw

Forelimb

**SKULL AND
MANDIBLE OF
STYRACOSAURUS**

Epoccipital bone

Nose horn core

Orbit

Naris

Mandible

**FOSSIL SKELETON OF
YOUNG HADROSAUR**

Scapula

Caudal vertebra

Phalanx

Orbit

**FOSSIL SKELETON
OF STRUTHIOMIMUS**

Femur

Pubis

Femur

Metatarsal

Metatarsal

Mandible

Tibia

Leathery skin

Shoulder spike

Eye

Mouth

Hindlimb

Forelimb

Hind foot

Forefoot

**EXTERNAL FEATURES
OF EUOPLOCEPHALUS**

THE VISUAL DICTIONARY *of*
DINOSAURS

Emerged hatchling

Eggshell

Nest material

MODEL OF ORODROMEUS NEST

Tail

Tail club

Stoddart

A DORLING KINDERSLEY BOOK

PROJECT ART EDITOR CLARE SHEDDEN
DESIGNER ELLEN WOODWARD

PROJECT EDITORS FIONA COURTENAY-THOMPSON, MARY LINDSAY
CONSULTANT EDITORS DAVID LAMBERT, DR RALPH E. MOLNAR
U.S. CONSULTANT LOWELL DINGUS (AMERICAN MUSEUM OF NATURAL HISTORY)
U.S. EDITOR CHARLES A. WILLS

MANAGING ART EDITOR STEPHEN KNOWLDEN
SENIOR EDITOR MARTYN PAGE
MANAGING EDITOR RUTH MIDGLEY

PHOTOGRAPHY ANDY CRAWFORD
ILLUSTRATIONS JOHN TEMPERTON, GRAHAM ROSEWARNE
MODEL MAKERS JOHN HOLMES, ROBY BRAUN, GRAHAM HIGH AND JEREMY HUNT (CENTAUR STUDIOS)

PRODUCTION HILARY STEPHENS

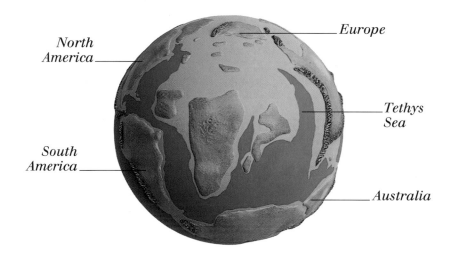

North America

Europe

Tethys Sea

South America

Australia

**THE EARTH DURING THE
CRETACEOUS PERIOD**

FIRST PUBLISHED IN CANADA IN 1993 BY STODDART PUBLISHING CO. LIMITED
34 LESMILL ROAD, TORONTO, CANADA, M3B 2T6
REPRINTED 1995

PUBLISHED IN GREAT BRITAIN IN 1993
BY DORLING KINDERSLEY LIMITED, 9 HENRIETTA STREET, COVENT GARDEN, LONDON WC2E 8PS

CANADIAN CATALOGUING IN PUBLICATION DATA
MAIN ENTRY UNDER TITLE:
THE VISUAL DICTIONARY OF DINOSAURS
CANADIAN ED.
INCLUDES INDEX.
ISBN 0-7737-2685-3

1. DINOSAURS – TERMINOLOGY – JUVENILE LITERATURE.
2. DINOSAURS – PICTORIAL WORKS – JUVENILE LITERATURE.
3. PICTURE DICTIONARIES, ENGLISH – JUVENILE LITERATURE.

QE862.D5V58 1993   j567.9'1'03   C92-095554-1

REPRODUCED BY COLOURSCAN, SINGAPORE
PRINTED AND BOUND BY ARNOLDO MONDADORI, VERONA, ITALY

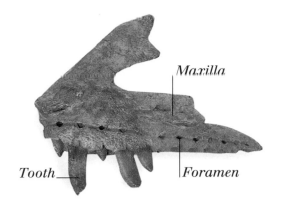

Maxilla

Tooth

Foramen

**UPPER JAW OF
TERATOSAURUS**

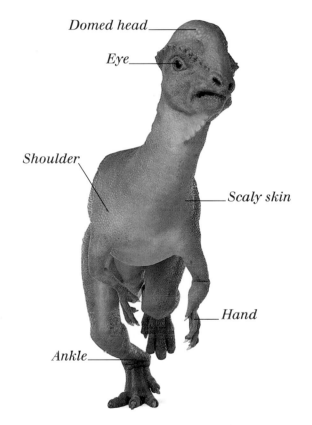

Domed head

Eye

Shoulder

Scaly skin

Hand

Ankle

**EXTERNAL FEATURES
OF STEGOCERAS**

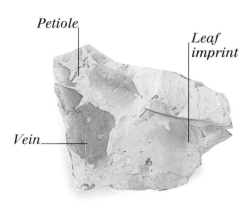

Petiole

*Leaf
imprint*

Vein

**FOSSILIZED LEAF OF
CRETACEOUS TREE**

Contents

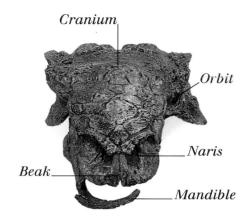

Cranium

Orbit

Naris

Beak

Mandible

**SKULL AND MANDIBLE
OF EUOPLOCEPHALUS**

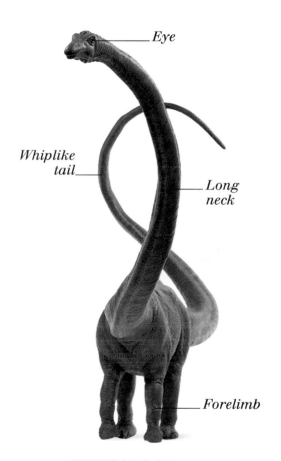

Eye

*Whiplike
tail*

*Long
neck*

Forelimb

**EXTERNAL FEATURES
OF BAROSAURUS**

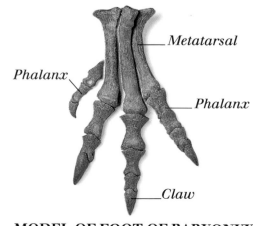

Metatarsal

Phalanx

Phalanx

Claw

MODEL OF FOOT OF BARYONYX

The dinosaurs

DINOSAURS WERE A LARGE GROUP OF REPTILES that were the dominant land vertebrates (animals with backbones) on Earth from the first part of the Late Triassic (231 million years ago) to the end of the Cretaceous period (65 million years ago). Dinosaurs were diverse, ranging from huge herbivores (plant-eaters) such as *Barosaurus*, which was 90 ft (27.4 m) long, to small carnivores (flesh-eaters) such as *Compsognathus*, which was less than 4 ft 8 in (1.4 m) long. Two features that most dinosaurs had in common were raised metatarsals and an erect stance. Their erect stance enabled dinosaurs to keep their bodies well above the ground, unlike the sprawling and semi-sprawling stances of other reptiles. Dinosaurs can be categorized into two main groups according to the structure of their pelvis (hip bones): ornithischian (bird-hipped) and saurischian (lizard-hipped) dinosaurs. Ornithischians had a relatively long, shallow ilium and a backward-slanting pubis. Most saurischians had a shorter, deeper ilium and a forward-slanting pubis. A third, small group of dinosaurs, the herrerasaurs, had pelvic bones similar to those of saurischians.

BAROSAURUS
A saurischian dinosaur

COMPARISON OF ANIMAL STANCES

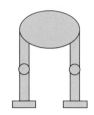

ERECT STANCE
The thighs and upper arms project straight down from the body, so that the knees and elbows are straight.

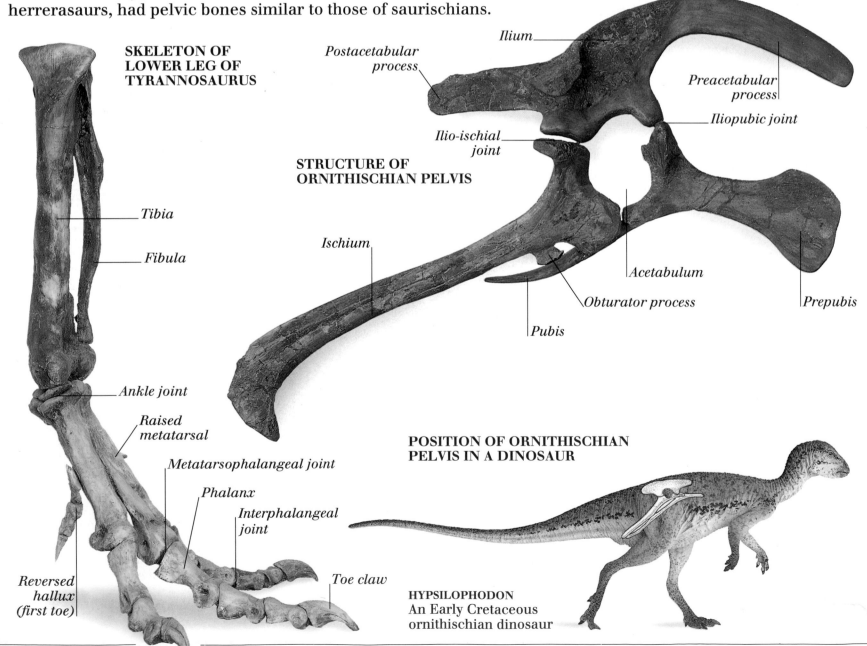

SKELETON OF LOWER LEG OF TYRANNOSAURUS

Tibia

Fibula

Ankle joint

Raised metatarsal

Metatarsophalangeal joint

Phalanx

Interphalangeal joint

Reversed hallux (first toe)

Toe claw

STRUCTURE OF ORNITHISCHIAN PELVIS

Ilium

Postacetabular process

Preacetabular process

Iliopubic joint

Ilio-ischial joint

Ischium

Acetabulum

Obturator process

Pubis

Prepubis

POSITION OF ORNITHISCHIAN PELVIS IN A DINOSAUR

HYPSILOPHODON
An Early Cretaceous ornithischian dinosaur

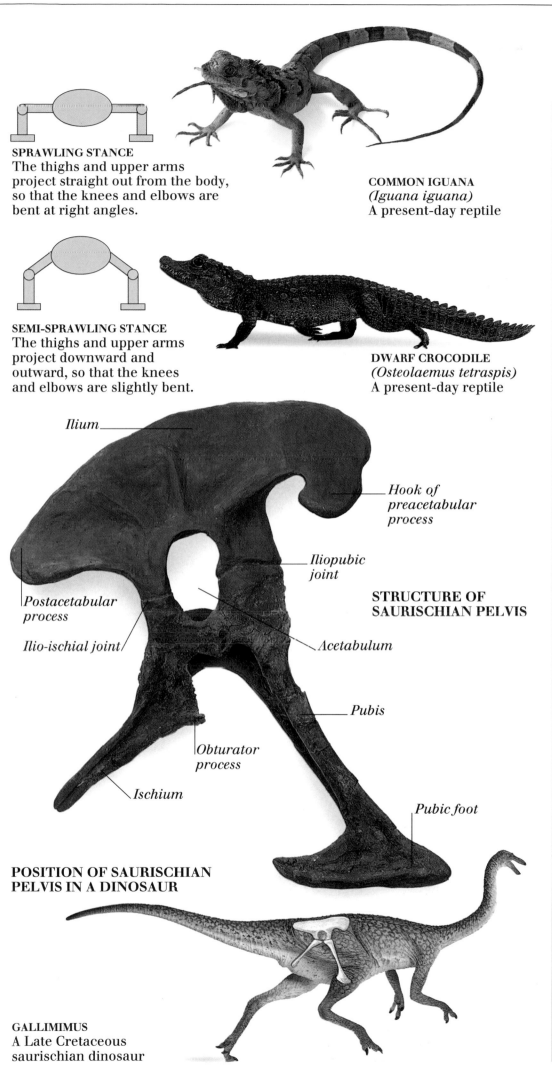

SPRAWLING STANCE
The thighs and upper arms project straight out from the body, so that the knees and elbows are bent at right angles.

COMMON IGUANA
(Iguana iguana)
A present-day reptile

SEMI-SPRAWLING STANCE
The thighs and upper arms project downward and outward, so that the knees and elbows are slightly bent.

DWARF CROCODILE
(Osteolaemus tetraspis)
A present-day reptile

STRUCTURE OF SAURISCHIAN PELVIS

Ilium

Hook of preacetabular process

Iliopubic joint

Postacetabular process

Ilio-ischial joint

Acetabulum

Pubis

Obturator process

Ischium

Pubic foot

POSITION OF SAURISCHIAN PELVIS IN A DINOSAUR

GALLIMIMUS
A Late Cretaceous saurischian dinosaur

THE GEOLOGICAL TIMESCALE

MYA	PERIOD		ERA
2	QUATERNARY		CENOZOIC
	TERTIARY		
65			
	CRETACEOUS		MESOZOIC
144			
	JURASSIC		
208			
	TRIASSIC		
248			
	PERMIAN		
286			
	CARBONIFEROUS	PENNSYLVANIAN (NORTH AMERICA)	
320		MISSISSIPPIAN (NORTH AMERICA)	
360			PALEOZOIC
	DEVONIAN		
408			
	SILURIAN		
438			
	ORDOVICIAN		
505			
	CAMBRIAN		
550			
	PRECAMBRIAN TIME		
4600			

Triassic period

CRETACEOUS 144-65 MYA	
JURASSIC 208-144 MYA	MESOZOIC ERA
TRIASSIC 248-208 MYA	

THE TRIASSIC PERIOD (248–208 million years ago) marked the beginning of what is known as the Age of the Dinosaurs (the Mesozoic era). During this period, the present-day continents were massed together, forming one huge continent known as Pangaea. This landmass experienced extremes of climate, with lush green areas around the coast or by lakes and rivers, and arid deserts in the interior. The only forms of plant life were nonflowering plants, such as conifers, ferns, cycads, and ginkgos; flowering plants had not yet evolved. The principal forms of animal life included primitive amphibians, rhynchosaurs ("beaked lizards"), and primitive crocodilians. Dinosaurs first appeared about 230 million years ago, at the beginning of the Late Triassic. The earliest known dinosaurs were the carnivorous (flesh-eating) herrerasaurids and staurikosaurids, such as *Herrerasaurus* and *Staurikosaurus*. Early herbivorous (plant-eating) dinosaurs first appeared in the Late Triassic and included *Plateosaurus* and *Technosaurus*. By the end of the Triassic, dinosaurs dominated Pangaea, possibly contributing to the extinction of many other reptiles.

TRIASSIC POSITIONS OF PRESENT-DAY LANDMASSES

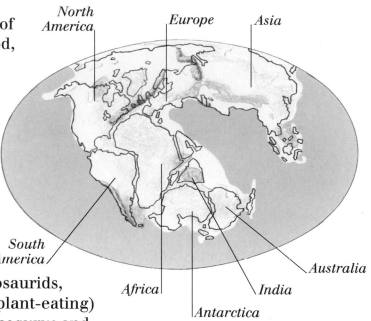

North America
Europe
Asia
South America
Africa
Antarctica
India
Australia

EXAMPLES OF TRIASSIC PLANT GROUPS

A PRESENT-DAY CYCAD
(*Cycas revoluta*)

A PRESENT-DAY GINKGO
(*Ginkgo biloba*)

A PRESENT-DAY CONIFER
(*Araucaria araucana*)

AN EXTINCT FERN
(*Pachypteris* sp.)

AN EXTINCT CYCAD
(*Cycas* sp.)

EXAMPLES OF TRIASSIC DINOSAURS

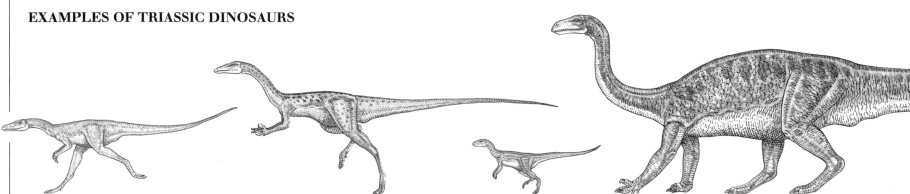

STAURIKOSAURUS
A staurikosaurid
Length: 6 ft 6 in (2 m)

COELOPHYSIS
A coelophysid
Length: 10 ft (3 m)

TECHNOSAURUS
A primitive ornithischian
Length: 3 ft 3 in (1 m)

PLATEOSAURUS
A plateosaurid
Length: 26 ft (7.9 m)

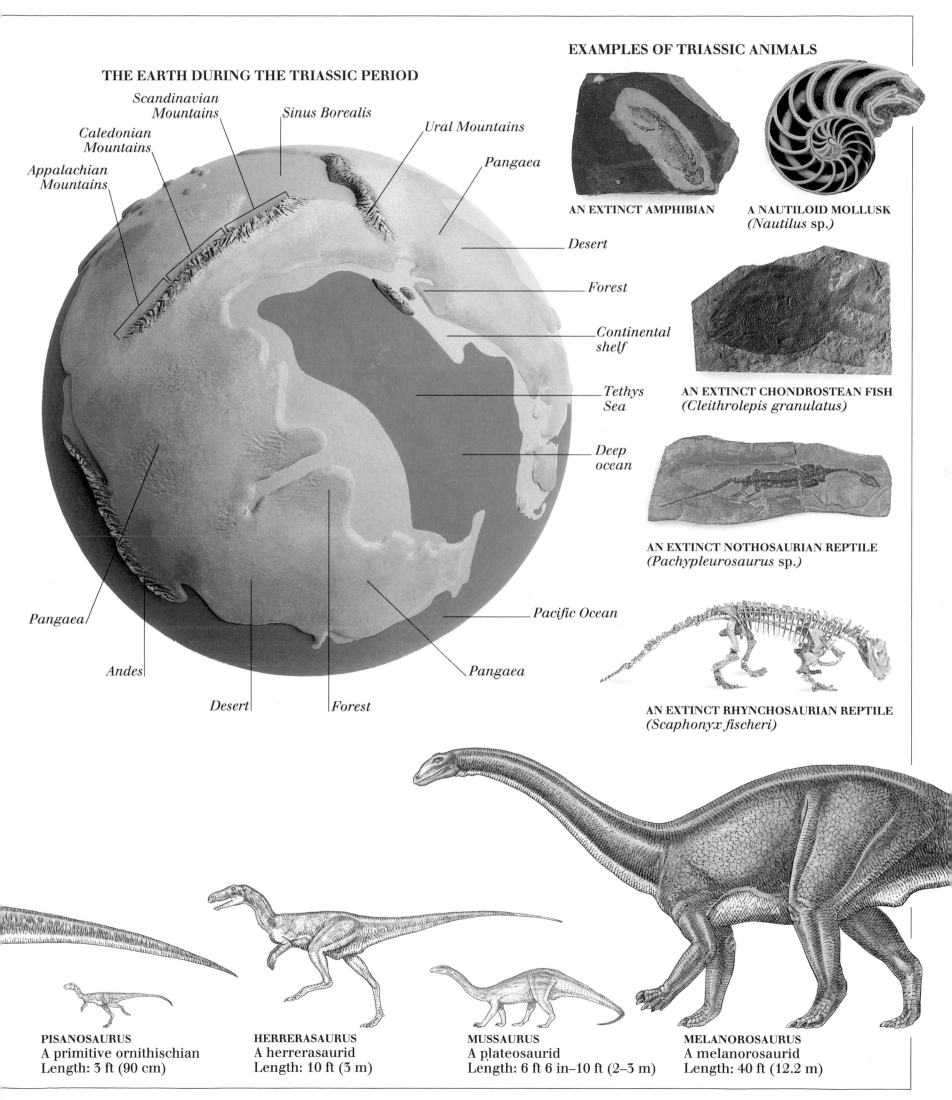

THE EARTH DURING THE TRIASSIC PERIOD

Caledonian
Mountains

Scandinavian
Mountains

Sinus Borealis

Ural Mountains

Appalachian
Mountains

Pangaea

Desert

Forest

Continental
shelf

Tethys
Sea

Deep
ocean

Pangaea

Andes

Desert

Forest

Pacific Ocean

Pangaea

EXAMPLES OF TRIASSIC ANIMALS

AN EXTINCT AMPHIBIAN

A NAUTILOID MOLLUSK
(*Nautilus* sp.)

AN EXTINCT CHONDROSTEAN FISH
(*Cleithrolepis granulatus*)

AN EXTINCT NOTHOSAURIAN REPTILE
(*Pachypleurosaurus* sp.)

AN EXTINCT RHYNCHOSAURIAN REPTILE
(*Scaphonyx fischeri*)

PISANOSAURUS
A primitive ornithischian
Length: 3 ft (90 cm)

HERRERASAURUS
A herrerasaurid
Length: 10 ft (3 m)

MUSSAURUS
A plateosaurid
Length: 6 ft 6 in–10 ft (2–3 m)

MELANOROSAURUS
A melanorosaurid
Length: 40 ft (12.2 m)

Jurassic period

CRETACEOUS 144-65 MYA	
JURASSIC 208-144 MYA	MESOZOIC ERA
TRIASSIC 248-208 MYA	

THE JURASSIC PERIOD, the middle part of the Mesozoic era, lasted from 208 to 144 million years ago. During the Jurassic, the landmass of Pangaea broke up into the continents of Gondwanaland and Laurasia, and sea levels rose, flooding areas of lower land. The Jurassic climate was warm and moist. Plants such as ginkgos, horsetails, and conifers thrived, and giant redwood trees appeared, as did the first flowering plants. The abundance of plant food led to the proliferation of herbivorous (plant-eating) dinosaurs, such as the large sauropods (e.g., *Diplodocus*) and stegosaurs (e.g., *Stegosaurus*). Carnivorous (flesh-eating) dinosaurs, such as *Compsognathus* and *Allosaurus*, also flourished by hunting the many animals, including other dinosaurs, that existed. Other Jurassic animals included shrewlike mammals, and pterosaurs (flying reptiles), as well as plesiosaurs and ichthyosaurs (both marine reptiles).

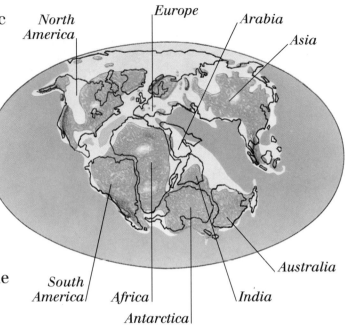

North America
Europe
Arabia
Asia
Australia
South America
Africa
India
Antarctica

EXAMPLES OF JURASSIC PLANT GROUPS

A PRESENT-DAY FERN
(Dicksonia antarctica)

A PRESENT-DAY HORSETAIL
(Equisetum arvense)

A PRESENT-DAY CONIFER
(Taxus baccata)

AN EXTINCT CONIFER

AN EXTINCT REDWOOD
(Sequoiadendron sp.)

EXAMPLES OF JURASSIC DINOSAURS

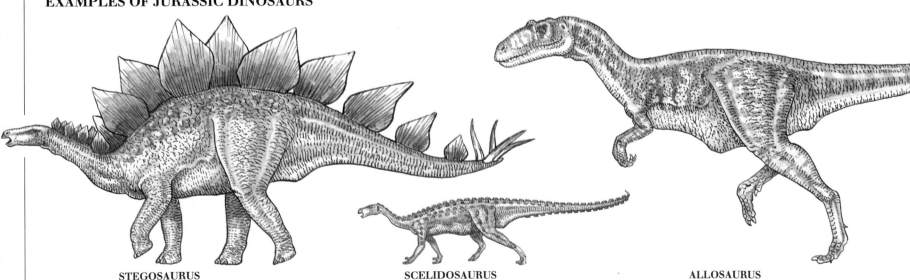

STEGOSAURUS
A stegosaurid
Length: 30 ft (9.1 m)

SCELIDOSAURUS
A scelidosaurid
Length: 13 ft (4 m)

ALLOSAURUS
An allosaurid
Length: 36 ft (11 m)

THE EARTH DURING THE JURASSIC PERIOD

Laurasia

Laurasia

North Atlantic Ocean

Ural Mountains

North American Cordillera

Turgai Strait

Forest

Laurasia

Desert

Tethys Sea

Deep ocean

Continental shelf

Desert

Andes

Forest

Gondwanaland

Gondwanaland

Pacific Ocean

EXAMPLES OF JURASSIC ANIMALS

AN EXTINCT PTEROSAUR
(*Rhamphorhynchus* sp.)

AN EXTINCT BELEMNITE MOLLUSK
(*Belemnoteuthis* sp.)

AN EXTINCT RHYNCHOSAURIAN REPTILE
(*Homeosaurus pulchellus*)

AN EXTINCT PLESIOSAUR
(*Peloneustes philarcus*)

AN EXTINCT ICHTHYOSAUR
(*Ichthyosaurus megacephalus*)

DRYOSAURUS
A dryosaurid
Length: 10–13 ft (3–4 m)

CAMPTOSAURUS
A camptosaurid
Length: 16–23 ft (4.9–7 m)

DIPLODOCUS
A diplodocid
Length: 88 ft (26.8 m)

11

Cretaceous period

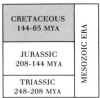

CRETACEOUS 144–65 MYA	
JURASSIC 208-144 MYA	MESOZOIC ERA
TRIASSIC 248-208 MYA	

THE MESOZOIC ERA ENDED WITH the Cretaceous period, which lasted from 144 to 65 million years ago. During this period, Gondwanaland and Laurasia were breaking up into smaller landmasses that more closely resembled those of the modern continents. The climate remained mild and moist, but the seasons became more marked. Flowering plants, including deciduous trees, replaced many cycads, seed ferns, and conifers. Animal species became more varied, with the evolution of new mammals, insects, fish, crustaceans, and turtles. Dinosaurs evolved into a wide variety of species during the Cretaceous; more than half of all known dinosaurs – including *Iguanodon*, *Deinonychus*, *Tyrannosaurus*, and *Hypsilophodon* – lived during this period. At the end of the Cretaceous, however, large dinosaurs became extinct. The reason for this mass extinction is unknown but it is thought to have been caused by climatic changes due to either a catastrophic meteor impact with the Earth or extensive volcanic eruptions.

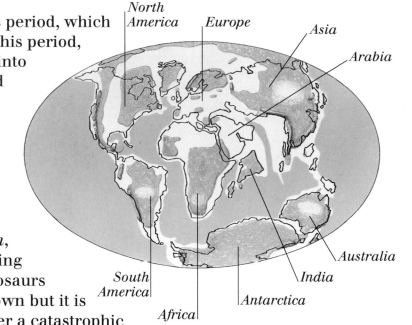

North America
Europe
Asia
Arabia
Australia
India
Antarctica
Africa
South America

EXAMPLES OF CRETACEOUS PLANT GROUPS

A PRESENT-DAY CONIFER
(Pinus muricata)

A PRESENT-DAY DECIDUOUS TREE
(Magnolia sp.)

AN EXTINCT FERN
(Sphenopteris latiloba)

AN EXTINCT GINKGO
(Ginkgo pluripartita)

AN EXTINCT DECIDUOUS TREE
(Cercidyphyllum sp.)

EXAMPLES OF CRETACEOUS DINOSAURS

IGUANODON
An iguanodontid
Length: 30 ft (9.1 m)

DEINONYCHUS
A dromaeosaurid
Length: 8–11 ft (2.4–3.4 m)

TYRANNOSAURUS
A tyrannosaurid
Length: 40 ft (12.2 m)

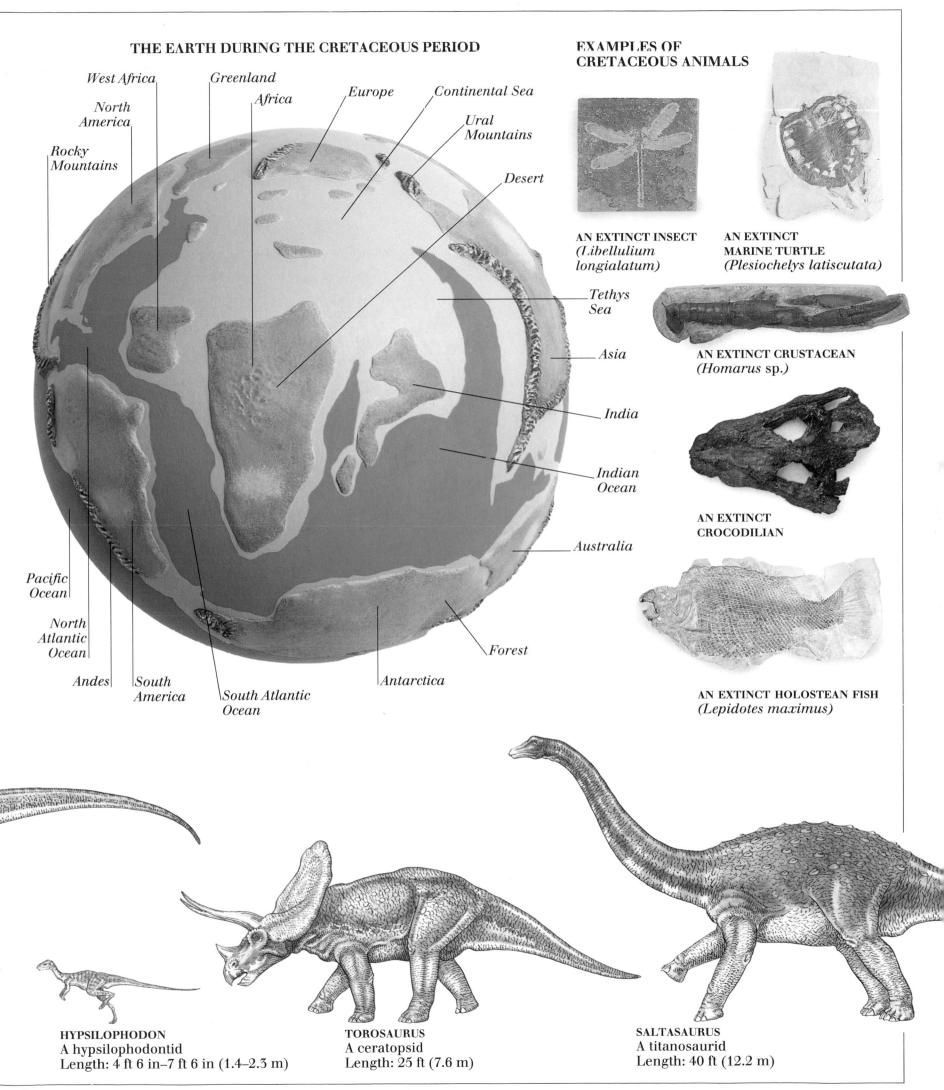

THE EARTH DURING THE CRETACEOUS PERIOD

West Africa
North America
Rocky Mountains
Greenland
Africa
Europe
Continental Sea
Ural Mountains
Desert
Tethys Sea
Asia
India
Indian Ocean
Australia
Forest
Antarctica
South Atlantic Ocean
South America
Andes
North Atlantic Ocean
Pacific Ocean

EXAMPLES OF CRETACEOUS ANIMALS

AN EXTINCT INSECT
(*Libellulium longialatum*)

AN EXTINCT MARINE TURTLE
(*Plesiochelys latiscutata*)

AN EXTINCT CRUSTACEAN
(*Homarus* sp.)

AN EXTINCT CROCODILIAN

AN EXTINCT HOLOSTEAN FISH
(*Lepidotes maximus*)

HYPSILOPHODON
A hypsilophodontid
Length: 4 ft 6 in–7 ft 6 in (1.4–2.3 m)

TOROSAURUS
A ceratopsid
Length: 25 ft (7.6 m)

SALTASAURUS
A titanosaurid
Length: 40 ft (12.2 m)

13

Small theropods

SMALL THEROPODS were a diverse group of lightweight, predatory, saurischian (lizard-hipped) dinosaurs that were widespread from Late Triassic to Late Cretaceous times (231–65 million years ago). This group included some of the smallest dinosaurs known; *Compsognathus* was one of the smallest, at about 28 in (70 cm) long, and even the largest small theropod, *Coelophysis*, was only 10 ft (3 m) long. Typical small theropods – for example, *Coelophysis*, *Ornitholestes*, and *Compsognathus* – had narrow jaws with sharp teeth; long, flexible necks; long tails; and long legs that enabled them to run fast. *Avimimus* was different from other small theropods because it had a toothless beak that resembled that of toothless theropods (see pp. 18-19).

PROCOMPSOGNATHUS

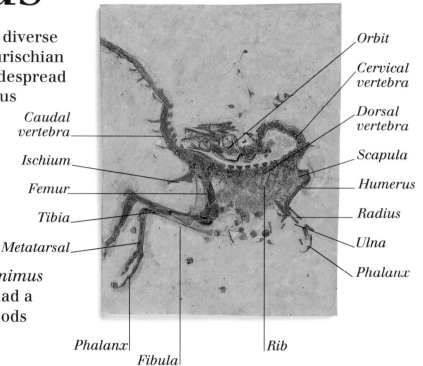

FOSSIL SKELETON OF COMPSOGNATHUS

Orbit
Cervical vertebra
Caudal vertebra
Dorsal vertebra
Ischium
Scapula
Femur
Humerus
Tibia
Radius
Metatarsal
Ulna
Phalanx
Phalanx
Rib
Fibula

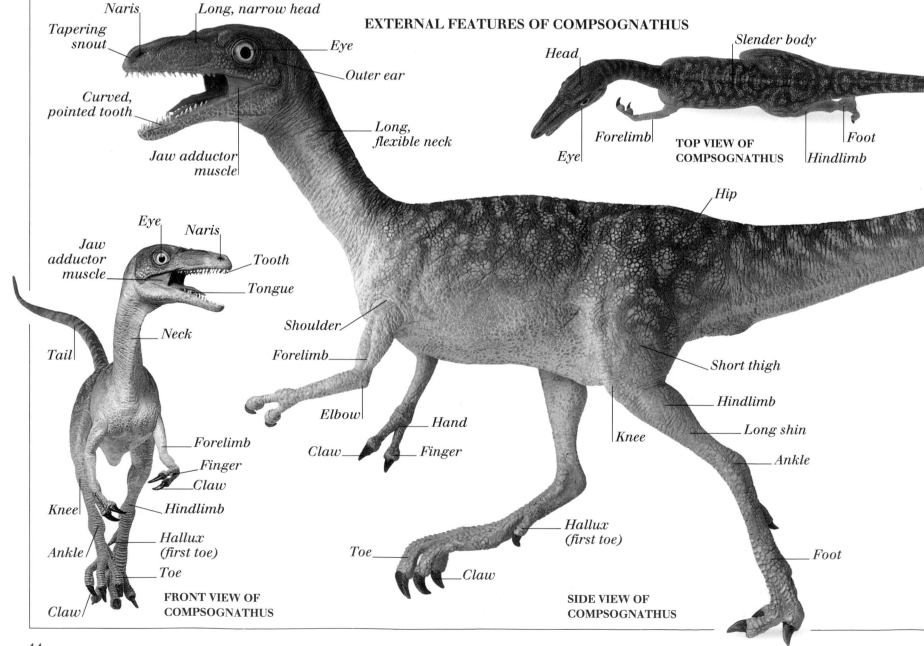

EXTERNAL FEATURES OF COMPSOGNATHUS

Naris
Long, narrow head
Tapering snout
Eye
Outer ear
Curved, pointed tooth
Long, flexible neck
Jaw adductor muscle

Head
Slender body
Forelimb
Foot
Eye
Hindlimb
TOP VIEW OF COMPSOGNATHUS

Hip

Eye
Naris
Jaw adductor muscle
Tooth
Tongue
Neck
Shoulder
Tail
Forelimb
Short thigh
Elbow
Hand
Hindlimb
Claw
Finger
Long shin
Forelimb
Knee
Finger
Claw
Ankle
Claw
Knee
Hindlimb
Hallux (first toe)
Ankle
Hallux (first toe)
Toe
Foot
Toe
Claw
Claw
FRONT VIEW OF COMPSOGNATHUS
SIDE VIEW OF COMPSOGNATHUS

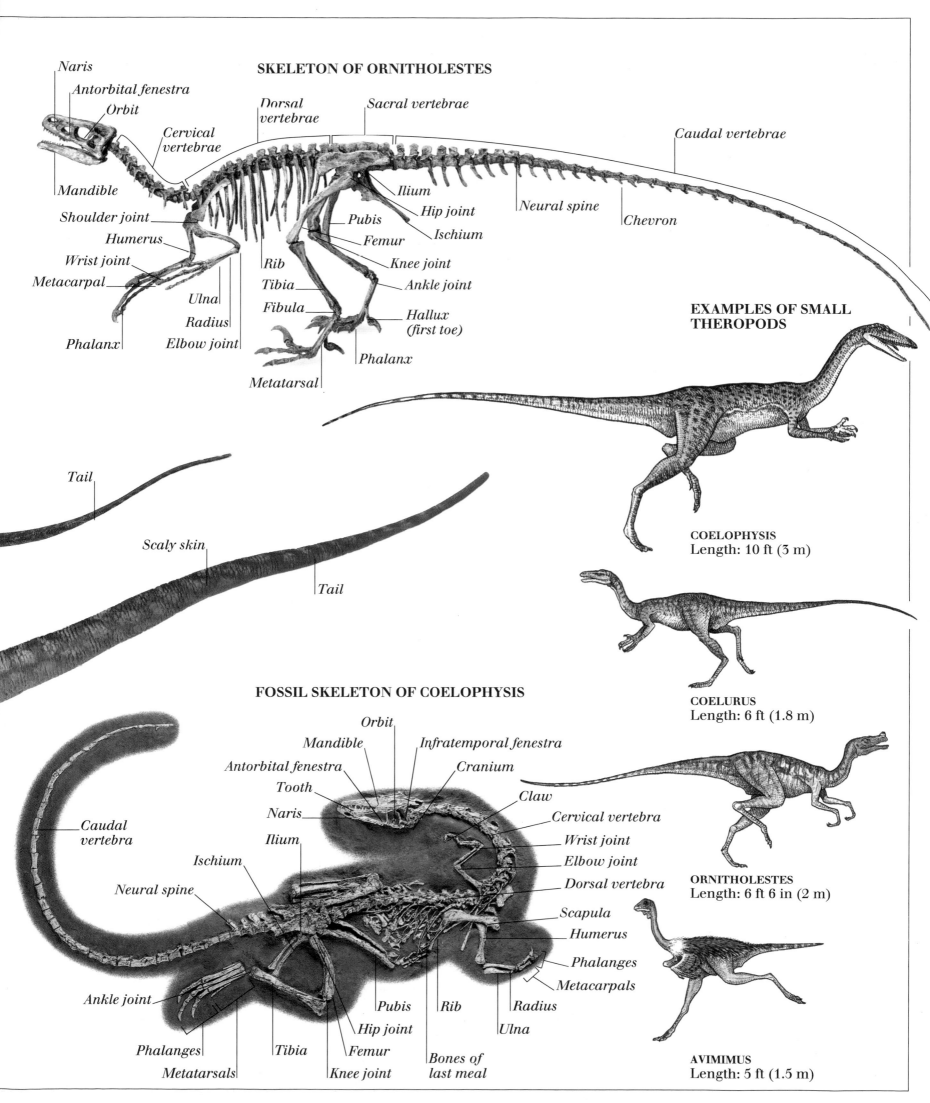

SKELETON OF ORNITHOLESTES

Naris

Antorbital fenestra

Orbit

Cervical vertebrae

Dorsal vertebrae

Sacral vertebrae

Caudal vertebrae

Mandible

Shoulder joint

Ilium

Hip joint

Neural spine

Chevron

Humerus

Pubis

Ischium

Femur

Wrist joint

Rib

Knee joint

Metacarpal

Ulna

Tibia

Ankle joint

Fibula

Hallux (first toe)

Radius

Phalanx

Elbow joint

Phalanx

Metatarsal

Tail

Scaly skin

Tail

EXAMPLES OF SMALL THEROPODS

COELOPHYSIS
Length: 10 ft (3 m)

COELURUS
Length: 6 ft (1.8 m)

FOSSIL SKELETON OF COELOPHYSIS

Orbit

Mandible

Infratemporal fenestra

Antorbital fenestra

Cranium

Tooth

Claw

Naris

Cervical vertebra

Caudal vertebra

Ilium

Wrist joint

Ischium

Elbow joint

Neural spine

Dorsal vertebra

Scapula

Humerus

Phalanges

Metacarpals

Ankle joint

Radius

Phalanges

Pubis

Rib

Ulna

Tibia

Hip joint

Metatarsals

Femur

Knee joint

Bones of last meal

ORNITHOLESTES
Length: 6 ft 6 in (2 m)

AVIMIMUS
Length: 5 ft (1.5 m)

15

Deinonychosaurs

DEINONYCHOSAURS WERE A GROUP of ferocious, predatory, saurischian (lizard-hipped) dinosaurs that lived in northern continents during the Cretaceous period (144–65 million years ago). The characteristic feature of these dinosaurs is a large, sickle-shaped claw on their second toe (deinonychosaur means "terrible claw lizard"). This claw flicked forward to slash prey during an attack. Deinonychosaurs were relatively small – ranging from about 6 ft (1.8 m) to 13 ft (4 m) in length – and agile, running on their powerful hindlegs and using their long, stiff tail to keep balance and also to help change direction quickly by acting as a rudder. It was thought that deinonychosaurs comprised two main subgroups – dromaeosaurids, such as *Deinonychus* and *Dromaeosaurus*, and troodontids, such as *Troodon* – but recent evidence suggests that dromaeosaurids and troodontids are not as closely related as previously believed. Dromaeosaurids had eyes at the side of the head, giving them a wide angle of vision. Their "terrible claws" were large. By hunting in packs, dromaeosaurids may have brought down prey much larger than themselves. By contrast, troodontids had smaller "terrible claws" and large, forward-facing eyes, which may have given them three-dimensional vision. Troodontids had larger brains, relative to their body size, than those of any other known dinosaur.

FOOT OF DEINONYCHUS

"Terrible claw" in resting position

Metatarsal

"Terrible claw"

Arc of claw movement

Enlarged joint

Phalanx

"Terrible claw" in flexed position

Claw

MOVEMENT OF "TERRIBLE CLAW"

SKELETON OF FOOT

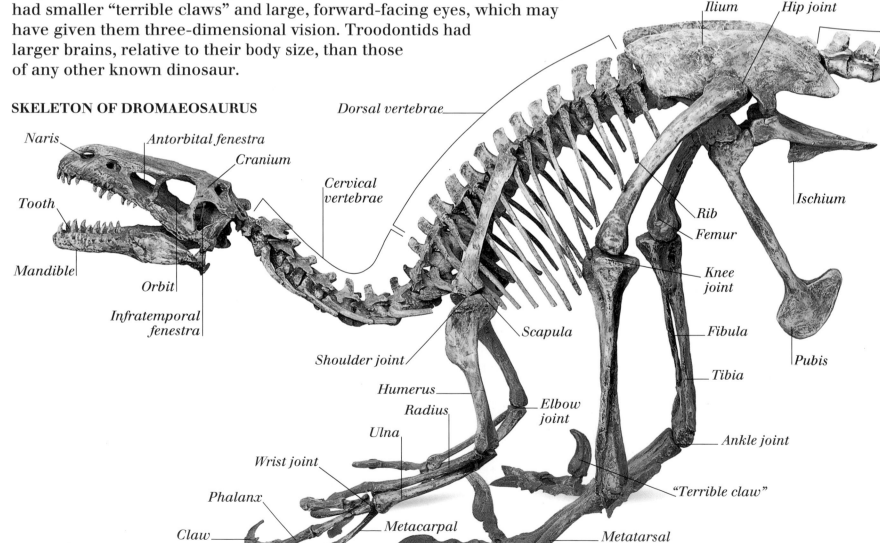

SKELETON OF DROMAEOSAURUS

Naris

Antorbital fenestra

Cranium

Tooth

Mandible

Orbit

Infratemporal fenestra

Dorsal vertebrae

Cervical vertebrae

Ilium

Hip joint

Ischium

Rib

Femur

Knee joint

Scapula

Shoulder joint

Fibula

Pubis

Tibia

Humerus

Radius

Elbow joint

Ulna

Wrist joint

Ankle joint

Phalanx

"Terrible claw"

Claw

Metacarpal

Metatarsal

Claw

Phalanx

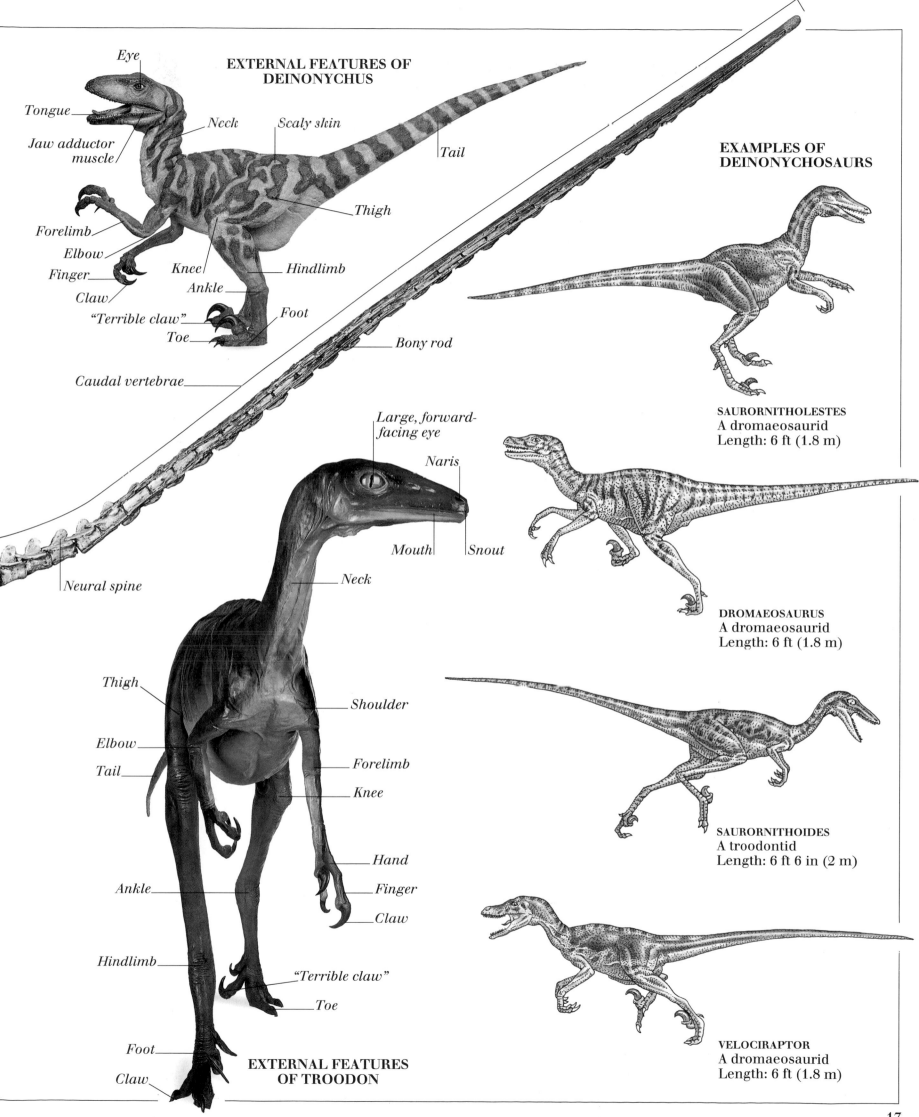

EXTERNAL FEATURES OF DEINONYCHUS

Eye

Tongue

Jaw adductor muscle

Neck

Scaly skin

Tail

Thigh

Forelimb

Elbow

Finger

Claw

Knee

Ankle

Hindlimb

"Terrible claw"

Toe

Foot

Bony rod

Caudal vertebrae

Neural spine

EXAMPLES OF DEINONYCHOSAURS

SAURORNITHOLESTES
A dromaeosaurid
Length: 6 ft (1.8 m)

Large, forward-facing eye

Naris

Mouth

Snout

Neck

Thigh

Shoulder

Elbow

Forelimb

Tail

Knee

Hand

Finger

Claw

Ankle

Hindlimb

"Terrible claw"

Toe

Foot

Claw

EXTERNAL FEATURES OF TROODON

DROMAEOSAURUS
A dromaeosaurid
Length: 6 ft (1.8 m)

SAURORNITHOIDES
A troodontid
Length: 6 ft 6 in (2 m)

VELOCIRAPTOR
A dromaeosaurid
Length: 6 ft (1.8 m)

Toothless theropods

TOOTHLESS THEROPODS COMPRISED TWO MAIN SUBGROUPS OF saurischian (lizard-hipped) dinosaur: ornithomimosaurs and oviraptorosaurs. Both groups lived during Late Cretaceous times (97.5–65 million years ago) in what are now Asia, North America, and Africa. They had toothless beaks, in contrast to the small theropods (see pp. 14-15), which had jaws containing small, sharp teeth. Ornithomimosaurs (meaning "bird-mimic lizards"), such as *Gallimimus*, *Ornithomimus*, *Struthiomimus*, and *Dromiceiomimus*, had some features in common with the modern ostrich: a small head with a long, narrow beak, a long neck, and powerful hindlimbs. Oviraptorosaurs (meaning "egg-plundering lizards"), such as *Oviraptor* (see p. 32), also had ostrich-like features, but their beaks were short. The internal anatomy of ornithomimosaurs and oviraptorosaurs is thought to have resembled that of modern birds, with a gizzard (muscular stomach) for grinding up food.

Eye

Toothless beak

SKULL AND MANDIBLE OF DROMICEIOMIMUS

Antorbital fenestra

Maxilla

Naris

Mandible

Mandibular fenestra

Orbit

Cranium

INTERNAL ANATOMY OF FEMALE GALLIMIMUS

Neural spine

Scapula

Lung

Gizzard

Rib

Dorsal vertebra

Ovary

Kidney

Ilium

Hip joint

Femur

Neural spine

Caudal vertebra

Cervical musculature

Trachea

Shoulder joint

Coracoid

Heart

Humerus

Posterior brachial muscle

Anterior brachial muscle

Claw

Anterior antebrachial muscle

Ulna

Posterior antebrachial muscle

Metacarpal

Liver

Intestine

Pubis

Femoral musculature

Tibia

Anterior crural muscle

Chevron

Cloaca

Ischium

Posterior crural muscle

Fibula

Tarsal

Metatarsal

Tendon

Phalanx

Toothless beak

Neck

Scaly skin

Tail

Elbow

Hand

Claw

Foot

Ankle

EXTERNAL FEATURES OF GALLIMIMUS

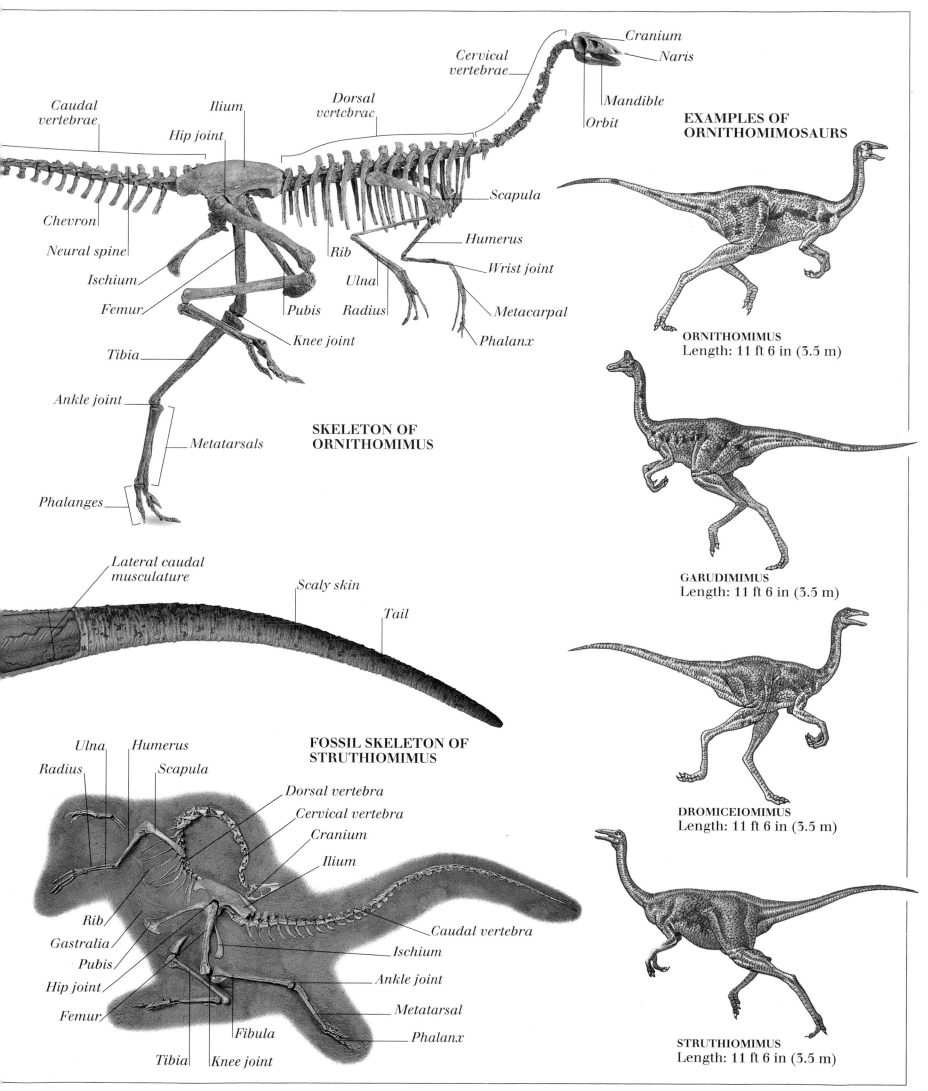

Caudal
vertebrae

Ilium

Dorsal
vertebrae

Cervical
vertebrae

Cranium

Naris

Hip joint

Mandible

Orbit

Chevron

EXAMPLES OF
ORNITHOMIMOSAURS

Neural spine

Scapula

Ischium

Humerus

Femur

Rib

Wrist joint

Pubis

Ulna

Radius

Metacarpal

Knee joint

Phalanx

Tibia

ORNITHOMIMUS
Length: 11 ft 6 in (3.5 m)

Ankle joint

Metatarsals

SKELETON OF
ORNITHOMIMUS

Phalanges

Lateral caudal
musculature

Scaly skin

GARUDIMIMUS
Length: 11 ft 6 in (3.5 m)

Tail

Ulna

Humerus

FOSSIL SKELETON OF
STRUTHIOMIMUS

Radius

Scapula

Dorsal vertebra

Cervical vertebra

Cranium

Ilium

DROMICEIOMIMUS
Length: 11 ft 6 in (3.5 m)

Rib

Gastralia

Caudal vertebra

Pubis

Ischium

Hip joint

Ankle joint

Femur

Metatarsal

Tibia

Fibula

Knee joint

Phalanx

STRUTHIOMIMUS
Length: 11 ft 6 in (3.5 m)

Carnosaurs 1

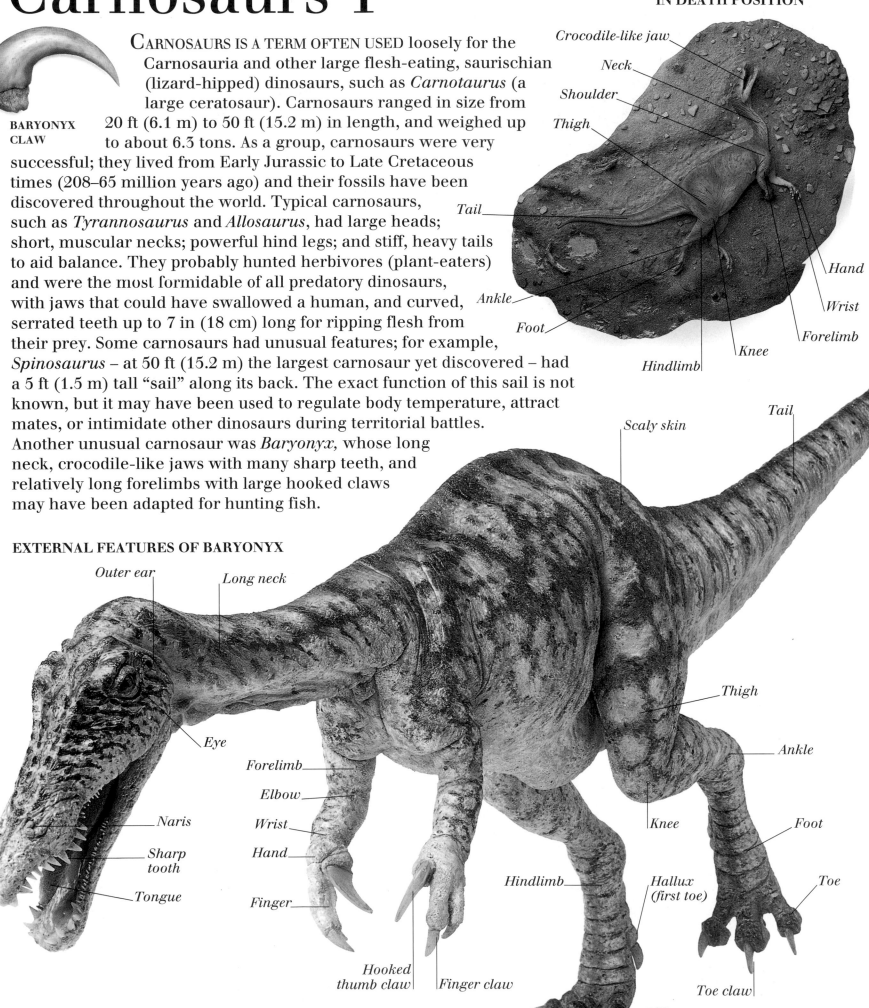

BARYONYX CLAW

CARNOSAURS IS A TERM OFTEN USED loosely for the Carnosauria and other large flesh-eating, saurischian (lizard-hipped) dinosaurs, such as *Carnotaurus* (a large ceratosaur). Carnosaurs ranged in size from 20 ft (6.1 m) to 50 ft (15.2 m) in length, and weighed up to about 6.3 tons. As a group, carnosaurs were very successful; they lived from Early Jurassic to Late Cretaceous times (208–65 million years ago) and their fossils have been discovered throughout the world. Typical carnosaurs, such as *Tyrannosaurus* and *Allosaurus*, had large heads; short, muscular necks; powerful hind legs; and stiff, heavy tails to aid balance. They probably hunted herbivores (plant-eaters) and were the most formidable of all predatory dinosaurs, with jaws that could have swallowed a human, and curved, serrated teeth up to 7 in (18 cm) long for ripping flesh from their prey. Some carnosaurs had unusual features; for example, *Spinosaurus* – at 50 ft (15.2 m) the largest carnosaur yet discovered – had a 5 ft (1.5 m) tall "sail" along its back. The exact function of this sail is not known, but it may have been used to regulate body temperature, attract mates, or intimidate other dinosaurs during territorial battles. Another unusual carnosaur was *Baryonyx*, whose long neck, crocodile-like jaws with many sharp teeth, and relatively long forelimbs with large hooked claws may have been adapted for hunting fish.

MODEL OF BARYONYX IN DEATH POSITION

Crocodile-like jaw

Neck

Shoulder

Thigh

Tail

Hand

Wrist

Ankle

Forelimb

Foot

Knee

Hindlimb

EXTERNAL FEATURES OF BARYONYX

Outer ear

Long neck

Scaly skin

Tail

Thigh

Ankle

Eye

Forelimb

Elbow

Wrist

Hand

Knee

Foot

Naris

Sharp tooth

Tongue

Finger

Hindlimb

Hallux (first toe)

Toe

Hooked thumb claw

Finger claw

Toe claw

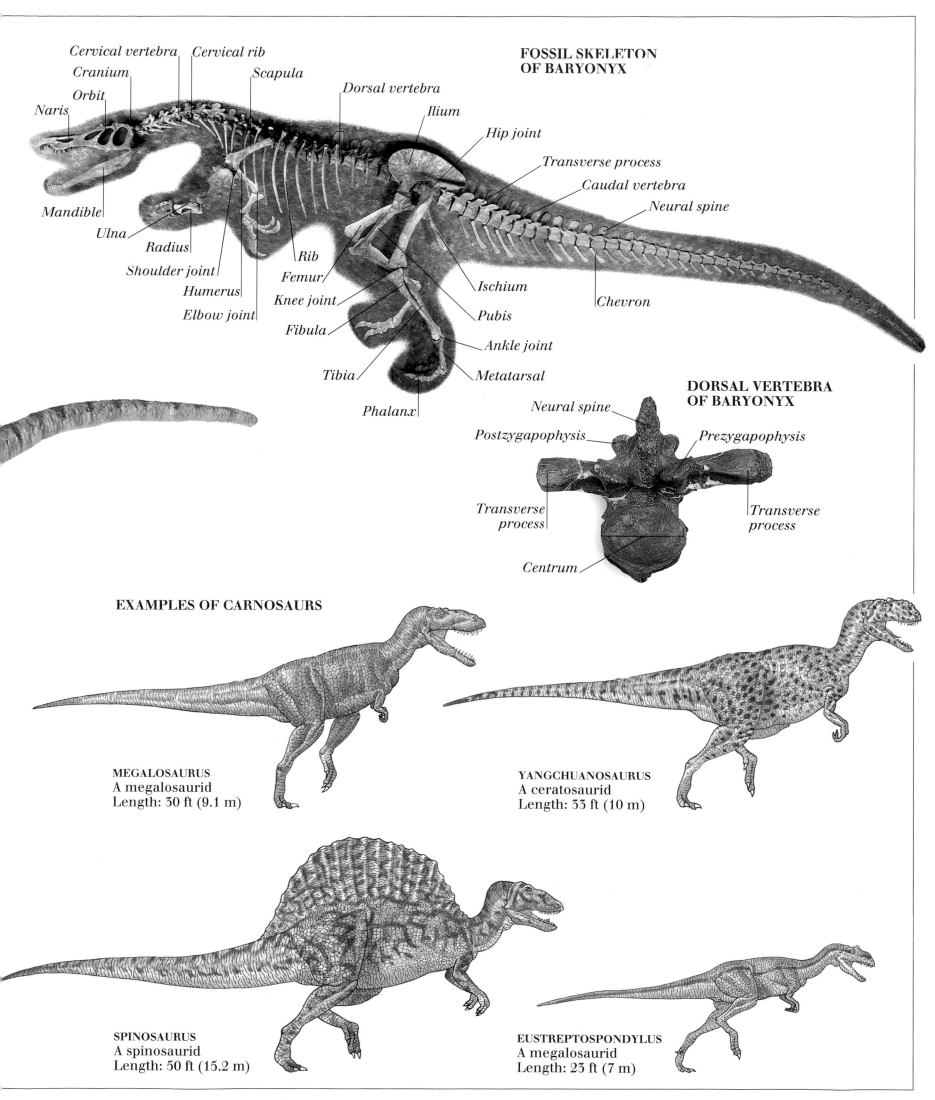

FOSSIL SKELETON OF BARYONYX

Naris

Cranium

Cervical vertebra

Orbit

Cervical rib

Scapula

Dorsal vertebra

Ilium

Hip joint

Transverse process

Caudal vertebra

Neural spine

Mandible

Ulna

Radius

Shoulder joint

Humerus

Elbow joint

Rib

Femur

Knee joint

Fibula

Tibia

Phalanx

Ischium

Pubis

Ankle joint

Metatarsal

Chevron

DORSAL VERTEBRA OF BARYONYX

Neural spine

Postzygapophysis

Prezygapophysis

Transverse process

Transverse process

Centrum

EXAMPLES OF CARNOSAURS

MEGALOSAURUS
A megalosaurid
Length: 30 ft (9.1 m)

YANGCHUANOSAURUS
A ceratosaurid
Length: 33 ft (10 m)

SPINOSAURUS
A spinosaurid
Length: 50 ft (15.2 m)

EUSTREPTOSPONDYLUS
A megalosaurid
Length: 23 ft (7 m)

Carnosaurs 2

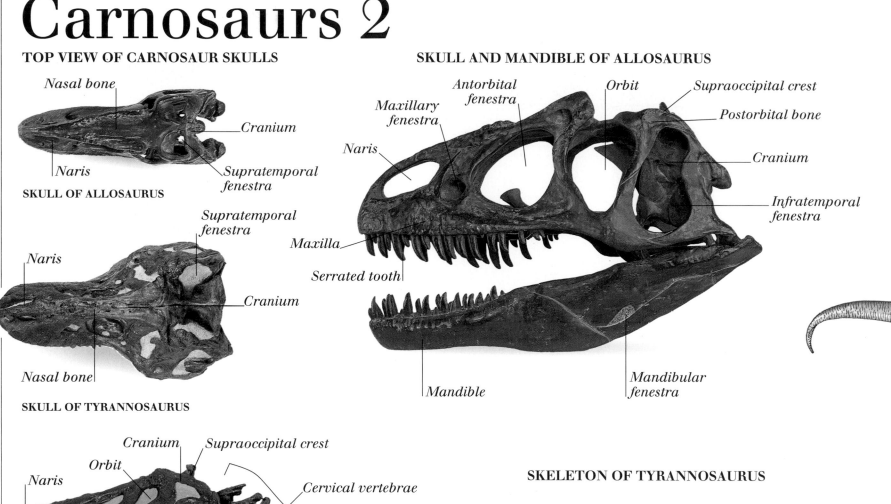

TOP VIEW OF CARNOSAUR SKULLS

Nasal bone

Cranium

Naris

Supratemporal fenestra

SKULL OF ALLOSAURUS

Supratemporal fenestra

Naris

Cranium

Nasal bone

SKULL OF TYRANNOSAURUS

SKULL AND MANDIBLE OF ALLOSAURUS

Antorbital fenestra

Maxillary fenestra

Orbit

Supraoccipital crest

Postorbital bone

Naris

Cranium

Maxilla

Infratemporal fenestra

Serrated tooth

Mandible

Mandibular fenestra

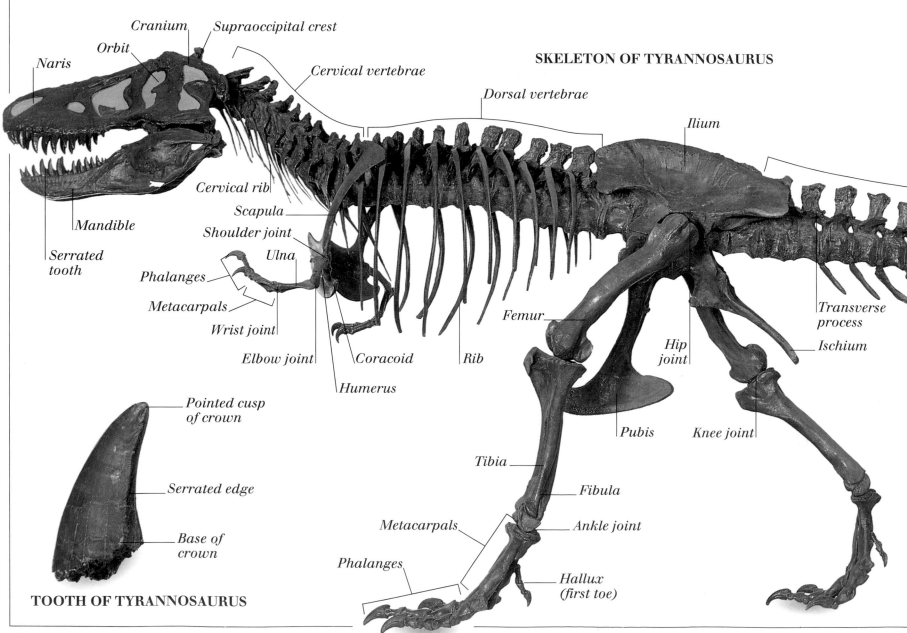

Cranium

Supraoccipital crest

Orbit

SKELETON OF TYRANNOSAURUS

Naris

Cervical vertebrae

Dorsal vertebrae

Ilium

Cervical rib

Scapula

Shoulder joint

Ulna

Mandible

Serrated tooth

Phalanges

Metacarpals

Transverse process

Wrist joint

Femur

Elbow joint

Coracoid

Rib

Ischium

Humerus

Pubis

Hip joint

Knee joint

Pointed cusp of crown

Tibia

Fibula

Serrated edge

Metacarpals

Ankle joint

Base of crown

Phalanges

Hallux (first toe)

TOOTH OF TYRANNOSAURUS

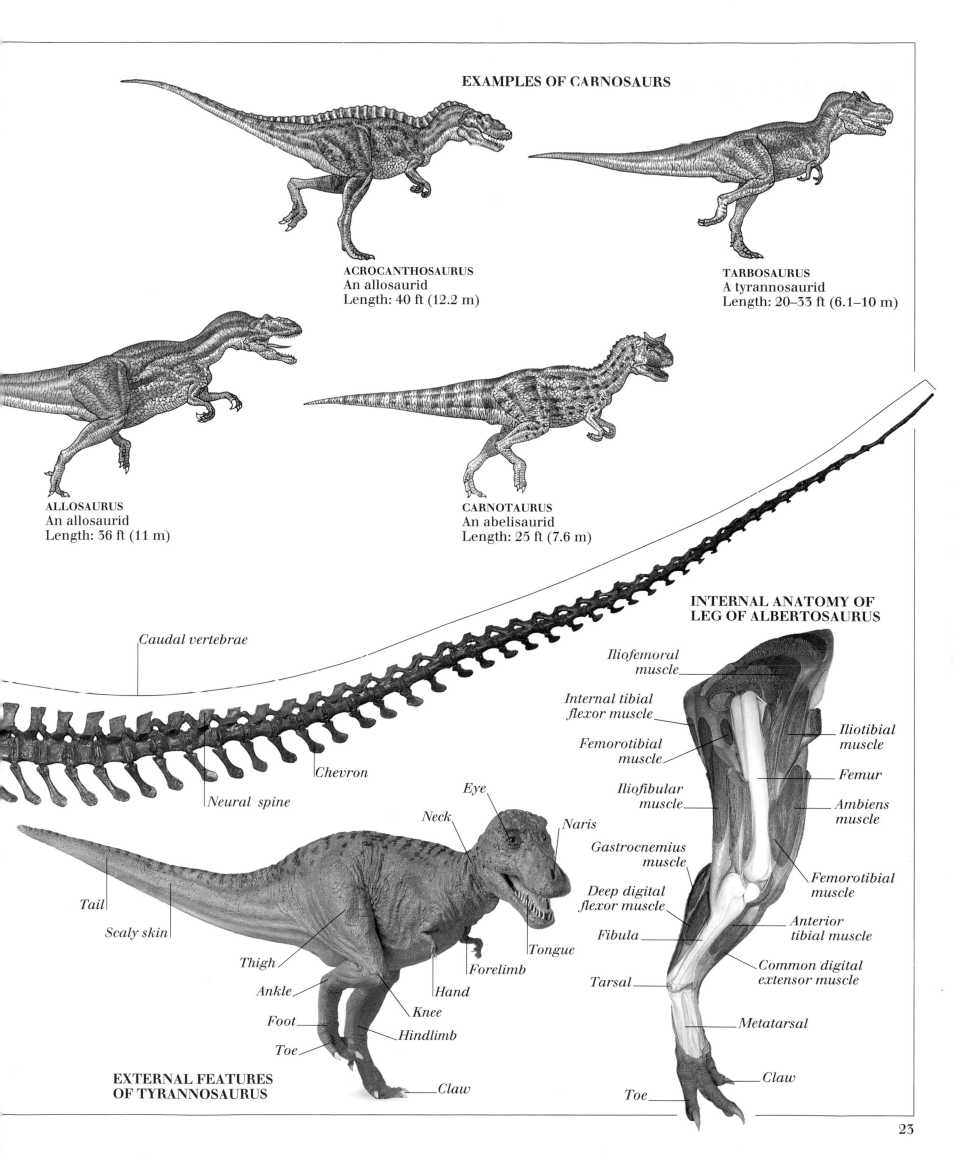

EXAMPLES OF CARNOSAURS

ACROCANTHOSAURUS
An allosaurid
Length: 40 ft (12.2 m)

TARBOSAURUS
A tyrannosaurid
Length: 20–33 ft (6.1–10 m)

ALLOSAURUS
An allosaurid
Length: 36 ft (11 m)

CARNOTAURUS
An abelisaurid
Length: 25 ft (7.6 m)

Caudal vertebrae

Chevron

Neural spine

**INTERNAL ANATOMY OF
LEG OF ALBERTOSAURUS**

Iliofemoral
muscle

Internal tibial
flexor muscle

Iliotibial
muscle

Femorotibial
muscle

Femur

Iliofibular
muscle

Ambiens
muscle

Gastrocnemius
muscle

Deep digital
flexor muscle

Femorotibial
muscle

Fibula

Anterior
tibial muscle

Common digital
extensor muscle

Tarsal

Metatarsal

Claw

Toe

Eye

Neck

Naris

Tail

Scaly skin

Tongue

Thigh

Forelimb

Ankle

Hand

Foot

Knee

Toe

Hindlimb

Claw

**EXTERNAL FEATURES
OF TYRANNOSAURUS**

23

Prosauropods

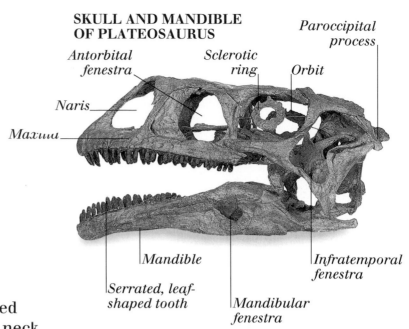

SKULL AND MANDIBLE OF PLATEOSAURUS

- *Antorbital fenestra*
- *Sclerotic ring*
- *Paroccipital process*
- *Orbit*
- *Naris*
- *Maxilla*
- *Mandible*
- *Infratemporal fenestra*
- *Serrated, leaf-shaped tooth*
- *Mandibular fenestra*

THECODONTOSAURUS

PROSAUROPODS WERE A group of saurischian (lizard-hipped) dinosaurs that lived from Late Triassic to Early Jurassic times (231–188 million years ago); they were distributed throughout the world. They are thought to have been the first large herbivorous (plant-eating) dinosaurs and may have had the same ancestors as sauropods (see pp. 26-29). Prosauropods varied considerably in size: *Anchisaurus* was one of the smaller prosauropods, at about 8 ft (2.4 m) long, and *Melanorosaurus* was one of the larger, at approximately 40 ft (12.2 m) long. Typical features of prosauropods included a small head containing leaf-shaped teeth, a relatively long neck and tail, and hindlimbs that were longer than the forelimbs; all known prosauropods had large, curved thumb claws.

SKELETON OF PLATEOSAURUS

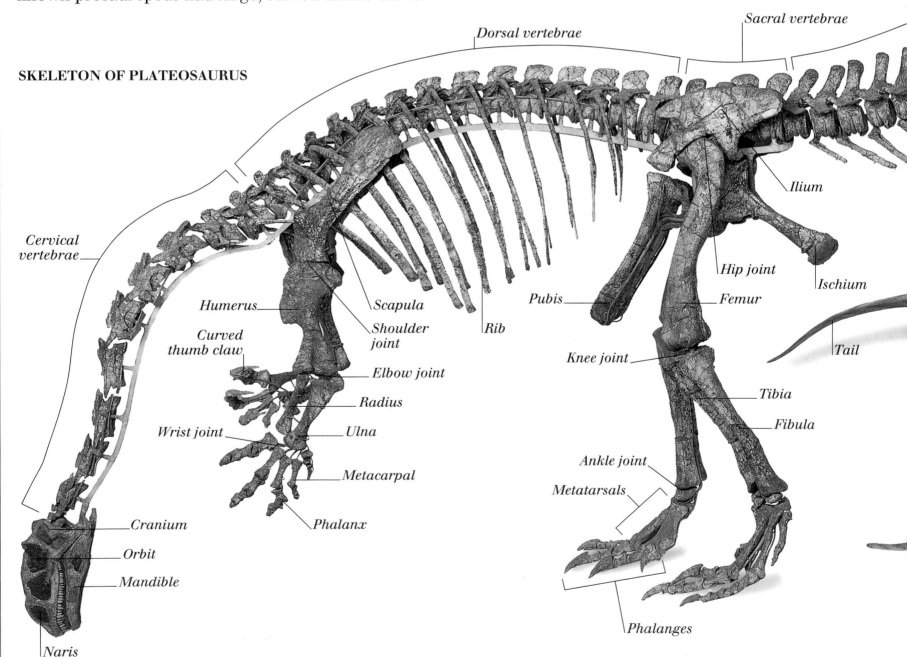

- *Dorsal vertebrae*
- *Sacral vertebrae*
- *Cervical vertebrae*
- *Ilium*
- *Humerus*
- *Scapula*
- *Hip joint*
- *Ischium*
- *Curved thumb claw*
- *Shoulder joint*
- *Pubis*
- *Femur*
- *Rib*
- *Elbow joint*
- *Knee joint*
- *Tail*
- *Radius*
- *Tibia*
- *Wrist joint*
- *Ulna*
- *Fibula*
- *Metacarpal*
- *Ankle joint*
- *Metatarsals*
- *Cranium*
- *Phalanx*
- *Orbit*
- *Mandible*
- *Phalanges*
- *Naris*

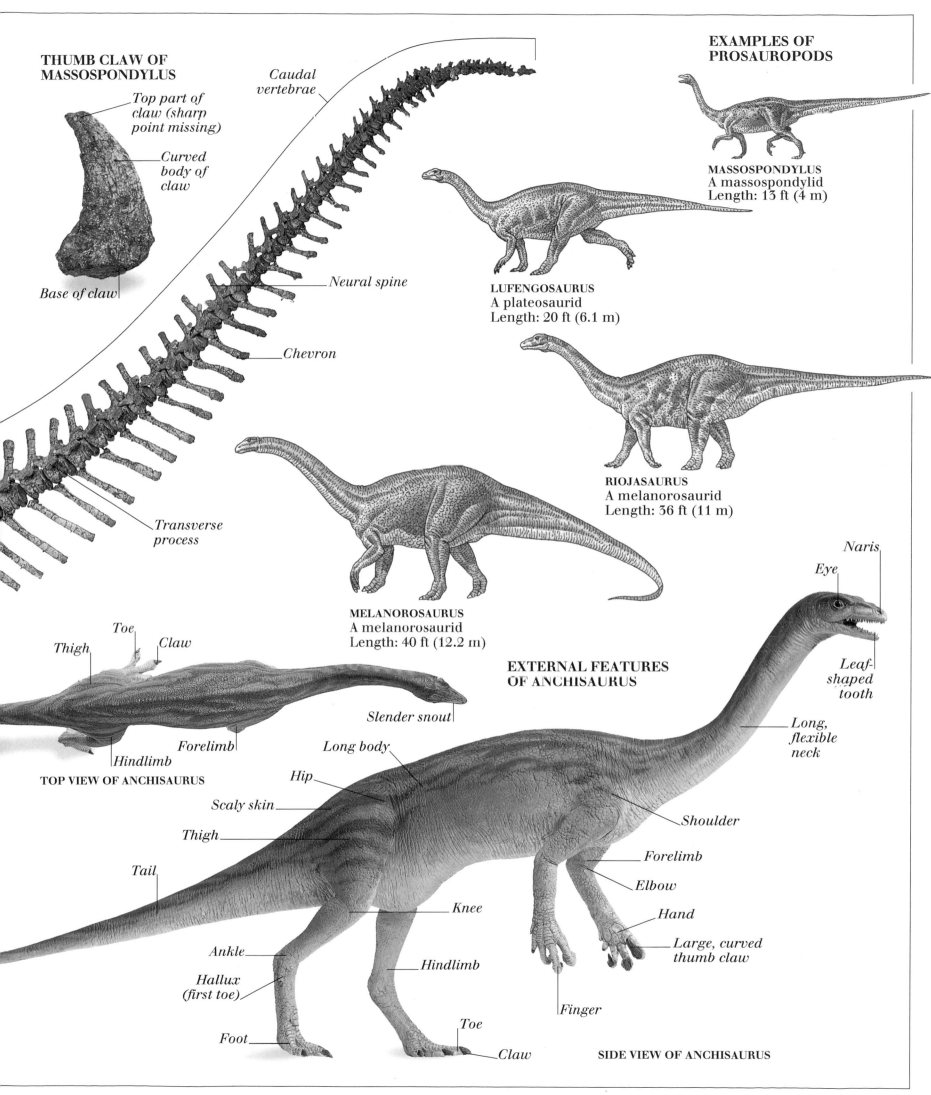

THUMB CLAW OF MASSOSPONDYLUS

Top part of claw (sharp point missing)

Curved body of claw

Base of claw

Caudal vertebrae

Neural spine

Chevron

Transverse process

EXAMPLES OF PROSAUROPODS

MASSOSPONDYLUS
A massospondylid
Length: 13 ft (4 m)

LUFENGOSAURUS
A plateosaurid
Length: 20 ft (6.1 m)

RIOJASAURUS
A melanorosaurid
Length: 36 ft (11 m)

MELANOROSAURUS
A melanorosaurid
Length: 40 ft (12.2 m)

Naris

Eye

Leaf-shaped tooth

Long, flexible neck

Thigh

Toe

Claw

Slender snout

Forelimb

Hindlimb

TOP VIEW OF ANCHISAURUS

EXTERNAL FEATURES OF ANCHISAURUS

Long body

Hip

Scaly skin

Thigh

Tail

Knee

Ankle

Hallux (first toe)

Foot

Hindlimb

Toe

Claw

Shoulder

Forelimb

Elbow

Hand

Large, curved thumb claw

Finger

SIDE VIEW OF ANCHISAURUS

25

Sauropods 1

SAUROPODS FORMED A large group of saurischian (lizard-hipped) dinosaurs that included some of the largest animals ever to have lived. *Brachiosaurus* was one of the heaviest, weighing up to 77 tons, which is more than the weight of 10 elephants. *Diplodocus* was one of the longest sauropods; measuring about 90 ft (27.4 m) from head to tail, it was almost as long as a blue whale, which, at about 100 ft (30.5 m), is the longest living animal. Sauropods supported their massive weight on pillar-like legs, which probably resembled those of elephants (see p. 28). As a group, sauropods were among the most successful dinosaurs: they were found throughout the world from Early Jurassic to Late Cretaceous times (208–65 million years ago). As well as being huge, sauropods typically had small heads; long, flexible necks; bulky bodies; and long tails. Some sauropods' bones were honeycombed with pleurocoels (hollows) to minimize weight. Sauropods were herbivores and, being so large, needed to eat vast amounts of vegetation. Consequently, their long necks – up to 49 ft (14.9 m) long in the case of *Mamenchisaurus* – were a great advantage, enabling them to reach vegetation that was too high up for other dinosaurs. Sauropods had no grinding teeth, which suggests that they swallowed food without chewing it; instead, food was probably ground up by gastroliths (stones) in the gizzard (muscular stomach).

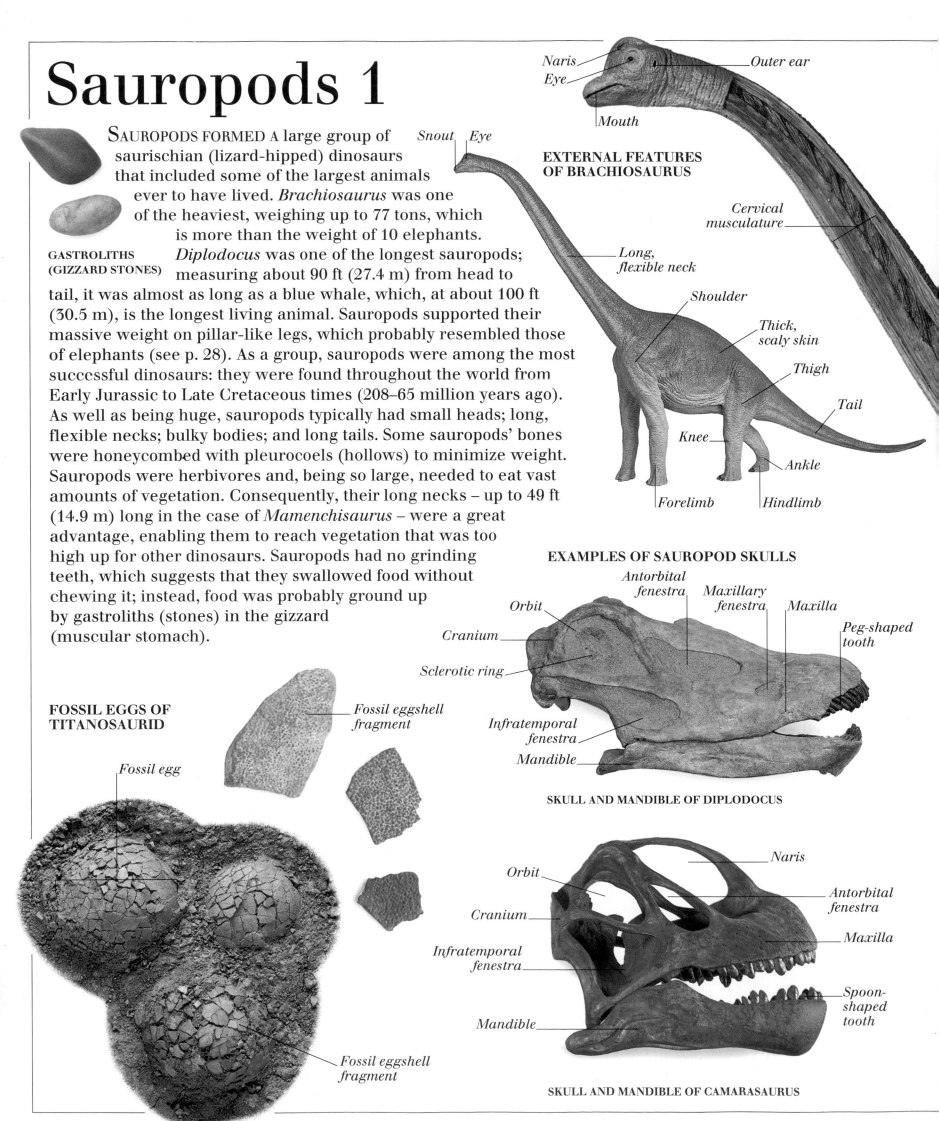

GASTROLITHS (GIZZARD STONES)

EXTERNAL FEATURES OF BRACHIOSAURUS

Naris
Eye
Outer ear
Mouth
Snout
Eye
Cervical musculature
Long, flexible neck
Shoulder
Thick, scaly skin
Thigh
Tail
Knee
Ankle
Forelimb
Hindlimb

EXAMPLES OF SAUROPOD SKULLS

Antorbital fenestra
Maxillary fenestra
Maxilla
Orbit
Cranium
Peg-shaped tooth
Sclerotic ring
Infratemporal fenestra
Mandible

SKULL AND MANDIBLE OF DIPLODOCUS

FOSSIL EGGS OF TITANOSAURID

Fossil eggshell fragment
Fossil egg
Fossil eggshell fragment

Naris
Orbit
Antorbital fenestra
Cranium
Maxilla
Infratemporal fenestra
Spoon-shaped tooth
Mandible

SKULL AND MANDIBLE OF CAMARASAURUS

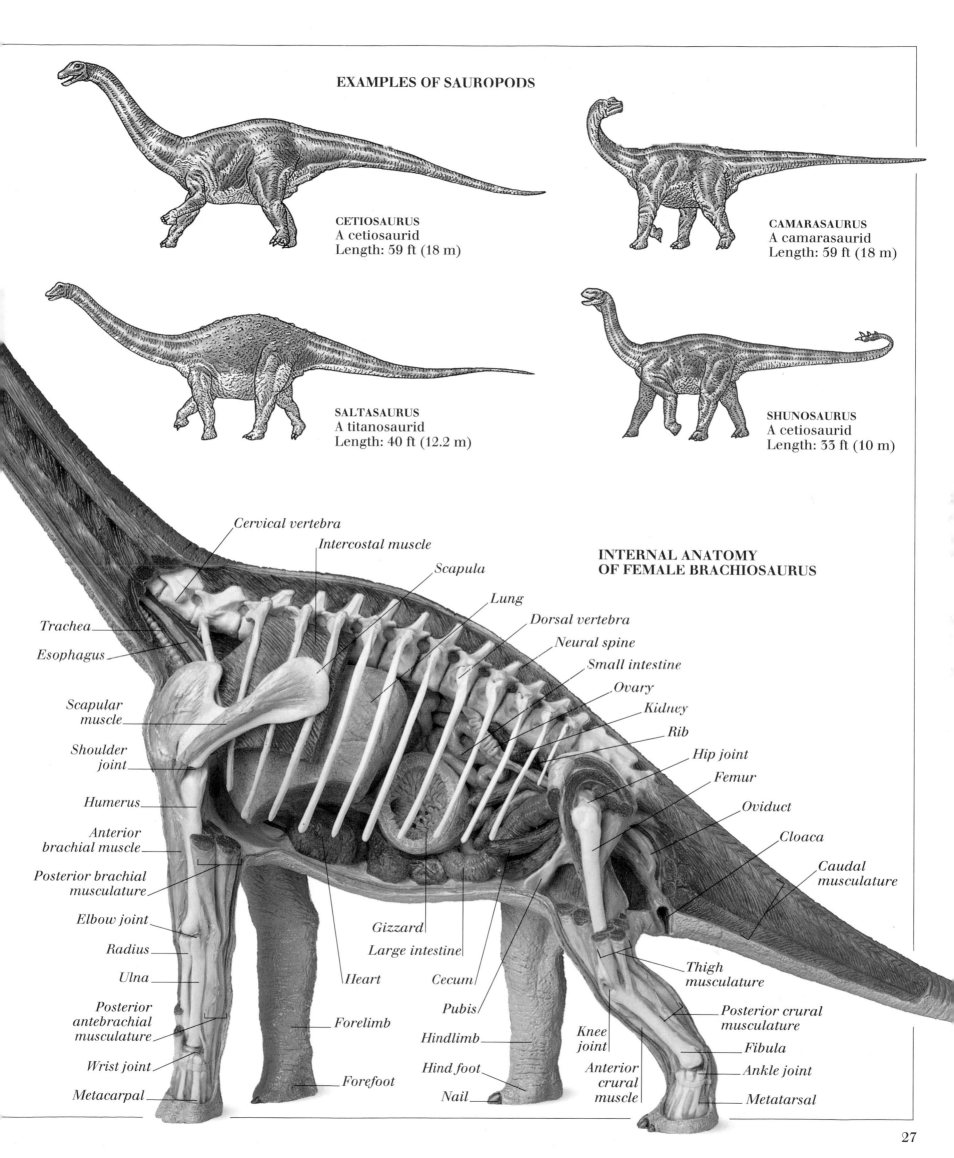

EXAMPLES OF SAUROPODS

CETIOSAURUS
A cetiosaurid
Length: 59 ft (18 m)

CAMARASAURUS
A camarasaurid
Length: 59 ft (18 m)

SALTASAURUS
A titanosaurid
Length: 40 ft (12.2 m)

SHUNOSAURUS
A cetiosaurid
Length: 33 ft (10 m)

INTERNAL ANATOMY OF FEMALE BRACHIOSAURUS

Cervical vertebra

Intercostal muscle

Scapula

Lung

Dorsal vertebra

Neural spine

Small intestine

Ovary

Kidney

Rib

Hip joint

Femur

Oviduct

Cloaca

Caudal musculature

Trachea

Esophagus

Scapular muscle

Shoulder joint

Humerus

Anterior brachial muscle

Posterior brachial musculature

Elbow joint

Radius

Ulna

Posterior antebrachial musculature

Wrist joint

Metacarpal

Heart

Large intestine

Gizzard

Cecum

Pubis

Forelimb

Forefoot

Hindlimb

Hind foot

Nail

Knee joint

Anterior crural muscle

Thigh musculature

Posterior crural musculature

Fibula

Ankle joint

Metatarsal

Sauropods 2

EXAMPLES OF CAUDAL VERTEBRAE OF BAROSAURUS

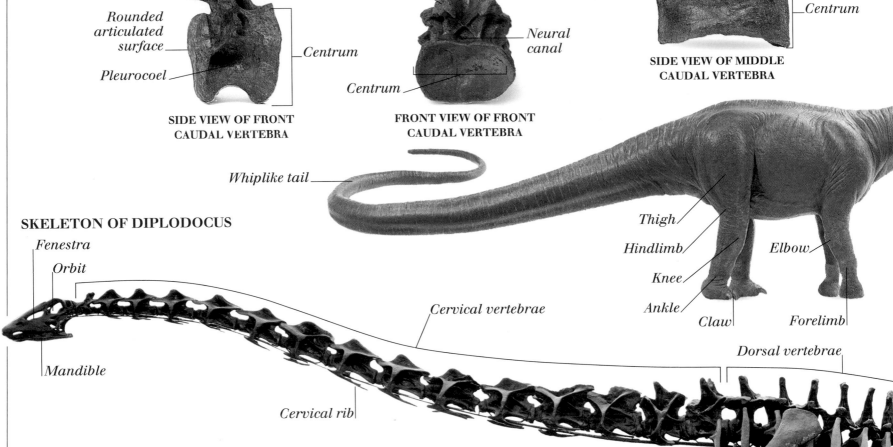

Neural spine

Postzygapophysis

Prezygapophysis

Rounded articulated surface

Centrum

Pleurocoel

SIDE VIEW OF FRONT CAUDAL VERTEBRA

Neural spine

Postzygapophysis

Prezygapophysis

Neural canal

Centrum

Centrum

FRONT VIEW OF FRONT CAUDAL VERTEBRA

Neural spine

Prezygapophysis

Postzygapophysis

Centrum

SIDE VIEW OF MIDDLE CAUDAL VERTEBRA

Whiplike tail

Thigh

Hindlimb

Knee

Ankle

Claw

Elbow

Forelimb

SKELETON OF DIPLODOCUS

Fenestra

Orbit

Mandible

Cervical rib

Cervical vertebrae

Dorsal vertebrae

Scapula

Coracoid

Rib

Humerus

Elbow joint

Radius

Ulna

Wrist joint

Metacarpals

Metacarpals

Knee joint

Fibula

Tibia

Phalanges

COMPARISON OF THE FOREFEET OF AN ELEPHANT AND DIPLODOCUS

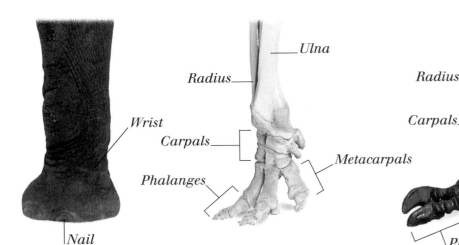

Wrist

Nail

FOREFOOT OF ELEPHANT

Ulna

Radius

Carpals

Phalanges

Metacarpals

FOREFOOT BONES OF ELEPHANT

Ulna

Radius

Carpals

Metacarpals

Phalanges

FOREFOOT BONES OF DIPLODOCUS

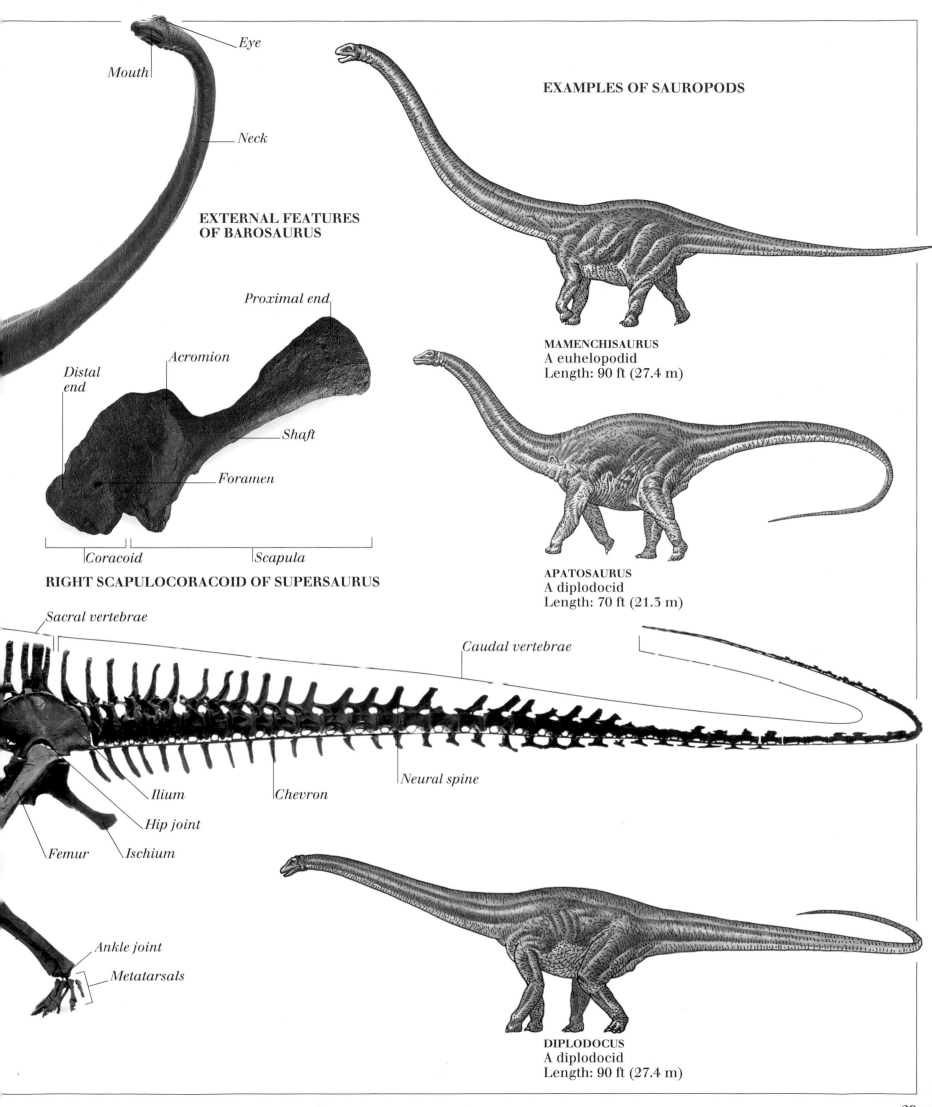

**EXTERNAL FEATURES
OF BAROSAURUS**

Mouth

Eye

Neck

EXAMPLES OF SAUROPODS

Proximal end

Acromion

Distal
end

Shaft

Foramen

Coracoid

Scapula

RIGHT SCAPULOCORACOID OF SUPERSAURUS

MAMENCHISAURUS
A euhelopodid
Length: 90 ft (27.4 m)

APATOSAURUS
A diplodocid
Length: 70 ft (21.3 m)

Sacral vertebrae

Caudal vertebrae

Ilium

Chevron

Neural spine

Hip joint

Femur

Ischium

Ankle joint

Metatarsals

DIPLODOCUS
A diplodocid
Length: 90 ft (27.4 m)

Herbivores' heads

HEAD OF GALLIMIMUS

HERBIVOROUS (PLANT-EATING) DINOSAURS probably spent much of their time eating. The wide range of vegetation consumed by the various herbivores may be reflected in the diversity of their heads, particularly of their jaws and teeth. For example, *Gallimimus* had a beak, possibly for cropping fruit and vegetation, *Anchisaurus* had ridged teeth for shredding the leaves from plants, *Stegosaurus* had a beak, and cheek teeth for grinding vegetation, and *Triceratops* had batteries of cheek teeth for slicing up plant food. The jaws of some herbivorous dinosaurs could move from side to side, which enabled them to grind up vegetation in their mouths. Other herbivores relied on gastroliths (stones) in their gizzard (muscular stomach) to break up the vegetation they had eaten. Most herbivorous dinosaurs had eyes at the sides of their heads, giving them a wide angle of vision so that they could spot predators approaching from any direction. Some herbivores had distinctive features on their heads. For example, *Triceratops* had massive brow horns, possibly for use in territorial battles, and hadrosaurs, such as *Brachylophosaurus*, had crests that distinguished one species from another within a herd.

SAUROPOD TEETH

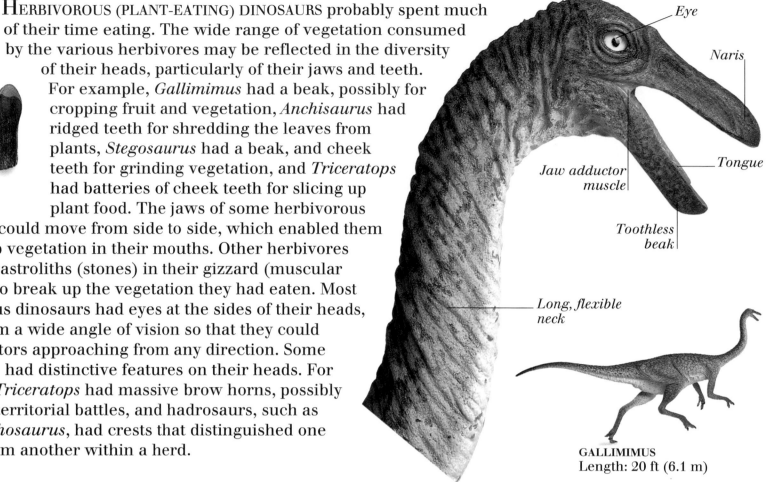

Eye

Naris

Tongue

Jaw adductor muscle

Toothless beak

Long, flexible neck

GALLIMIMUS
Length: 20 ft (6.1 m)

HEAD OF STEGOSAURUS

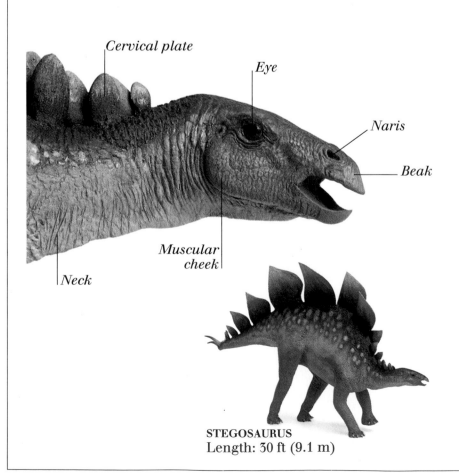

Cervical plate

Eye

Naris

Beak

Muscular cheek

Neck

STEGOSAURUS
Length: 30 ft (9.1 m)

HEAD OF ANCHISAURUS

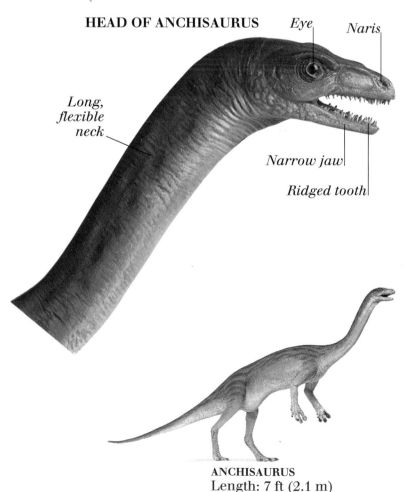

Eye

Naris

Long, flexible neck

Narrow jaw

Ridged tooth

ANCHISAURUS
Length: 7 ft (2.1 m)

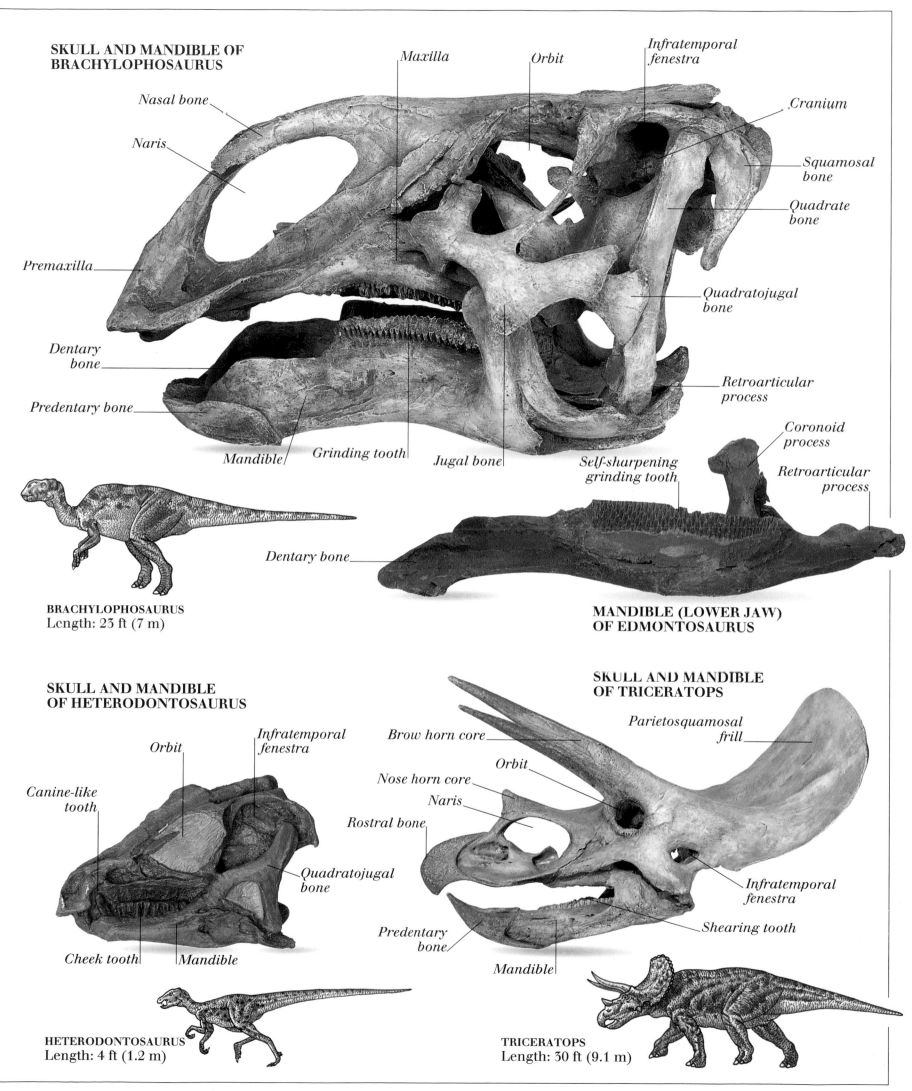

SKULL AND MANDIBLE OF BRACHYLOPHOSAURUS

Nasal bone

Naris

Maxilla

Orbit

Infratemporal fenestra

Cranium

Squamosal bone

Quadrate bone

Premaxilla

Quadratojugal bone

Dentary bone

Retroarticular process

Predentary bone

Coronoid process

Retroarticular process

Mandible

Grinding tooth

Jugal bone

Self-sharpening grinding tooth

BRACHYLOPHOSAURUS
Length: 23 ft (7 m)

Dentary bone

MANDIBLE (LOWER JAW) OF EDMONTOSAURUS

SKULL AND MANDIBLE OF HETERODONTOSAURUS

Orbit

Infratemporal fenestra

Canine-like tooth

Quadratojugal bone

Cheek tooth

Mandible

HETERODONTOSAURUS
Length: 4 ft (1.2 m)

SKULL AND MANDIBLE OF TRICERATOPS

Brow horn core

Parietosquamosal frill

Orbit

Nose horn core

Naris

Rostral bone

Infratemporal fenestra

Predentary bone

Shearing tooth

Mandible

TRICERATOPS
Length: 30 ft (9.1 m)

Carnivores' heads

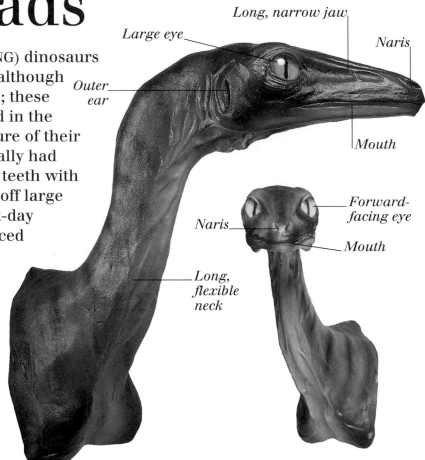

MOST CARNIVOROUS (FLESH-EATING) dinosaurs were probably active predators, although a few may have been scavengers; these flesh-eating life-styles are reflected in the features of their heads and the structure of their skulls. Carnivorous dinosaurs typically had strong jaws containing many sharp teeth with serrated edges to kill prey and tear off large chunks of flesh. As in many present-day carnivorous reptiles, the teeth of dinosaurs were replaced continually throughout their lifetime. Carnivorous dinosaurs did not have grinding teeth, which suggests that they swallowed food without chewing it. Some of their skulls had flexible joints, allowing them to distort slightly to accommodate huge mouthfuls of flesh. Typically, there were also many cavities in the skull, not only to minimize weight, but also to provide space for large, powerful jaw muscles. The heads and skulls of some carnivorous dinosaurs were adapted to specific diets. For example, *Baryonyx* had a crocodile-like skull that may have been adapted for catching fish, while *Oviraptor* had a deep, strong beak that might have been adapted for breaking into the shells of eggs or mollusks.

SKULL AND MANDIBLE OF DILOPHOSAURUS

HEAD OF TROODON

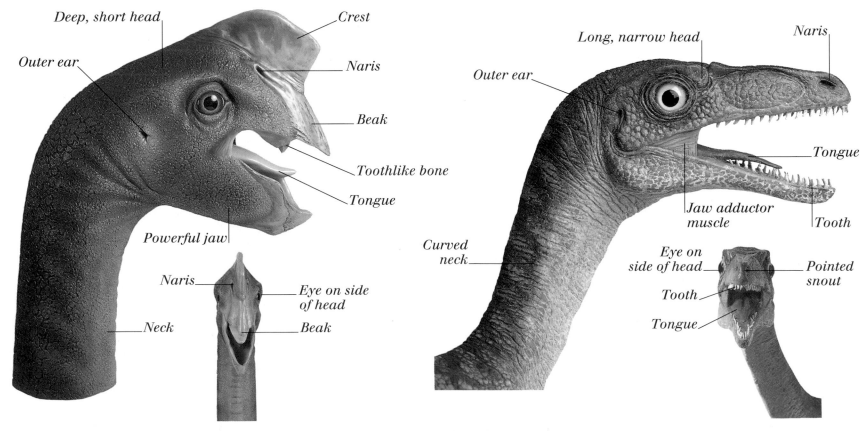

HEAD OF OVIRAPTOR

HEAD OF COMPSOGNATHUS

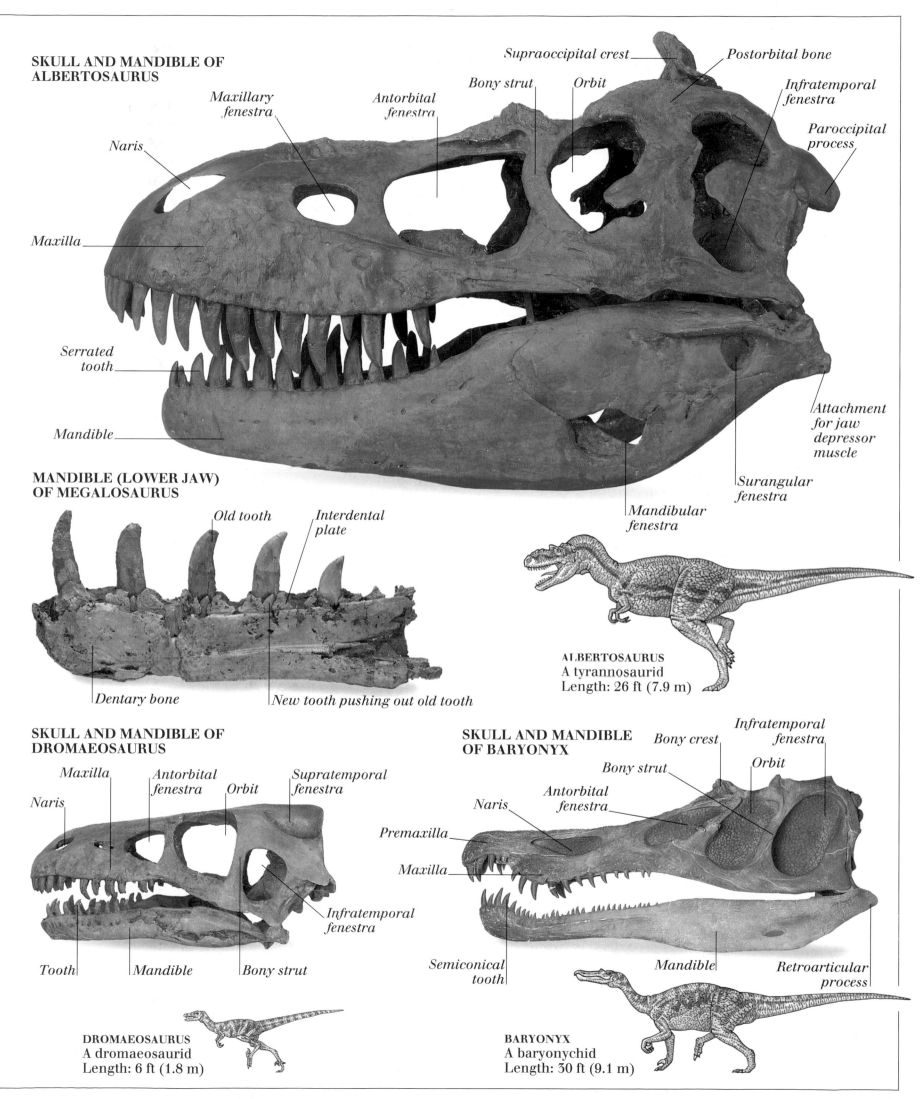

SKULL AND MANDIBLE OF ALBERTOSAURUS

Supraoccipital crest

Postorbital bone

Bony strut

Orbit

Infratemporal fenestra

Antorbital fenestra

Paroccipital process

Maxillary fenestra

Naris

Maxilla

Serrated tooth

Mandible

Attachment for jaw depressor muscle

Surangular fenestra

Mandibular fenestra

MANDIBLE (LOWER JAW) OF MEGALOSAURUS

Old tooth

Interdental plate

Dentary bone

New tooth pushing out old tooth

ALBERTOSAURUS
A tyrannosaurid
Length: 26 ft (7.9 m)

SKULL AND MANDIBLE OF DROMAEOSAURUS

Maxilla

Antorbital fenestra

Orbit

Supratemporal fenestra

Naris

Infratemporal fenestra

Tooth

Mandible

Bony strut

DROMAEOSAURUS
A dromaeosaurid
Length: 6 ft (1.8 m)

SKULL AND MANDIBLE OF BARYONYX

Infratemporal fenestra

Bony crest

Bony strut

Orbit

Antorbital fenestra

Naris

Premaxilla

Maxilla

Semiconical tooth

Mandible

Retroarticular process

BARYONYX
A baryonychid
Length: 30 ft (9.1 m)

Small ornithopods

SMALL ORNITHOPODS IS A GENERAL TERM for a varied collection of ornithischian (bird-hipped), herbivorous (plant-eating) dinosaurs that were widespread from Late Triassic to Late Cretaceous times (231–65 million years ago). Most of these dinosaurs were relatively small – typically less than about 13 ft (4 m) long. However, a few were considerably larger. For example, *Tenontosaurus* was about 21 ft (6.4 m) long. Large ornithopods, as their name suggests, were generally bigger than small ornithopods and included iguanodonts (see pp. 36-37) and hadrosaurs (see pp. 38-41). Most small ornithopods had the typical ornithischian arrangement of a toothless beak and cheek teeth for grinding up vegetation. However, the heterodontosaurids (meaning "different-tooth lizards") had three distinct types of teeth – sharp cutting teeth at the front, two pairs of long, canine-like teeth, and broad-ridged cheek teeth at the back of the mouth – an arrangement that is extremely unusual for herbivores of any kind.

EXAMPLES OF SMALL ORNITHOPODS

ORODROMEUS
A hypsilophodontid
Length: 8 ft (2.4 m)

INTERNAL ANATOMY OF MALE HYPSILOPHODON

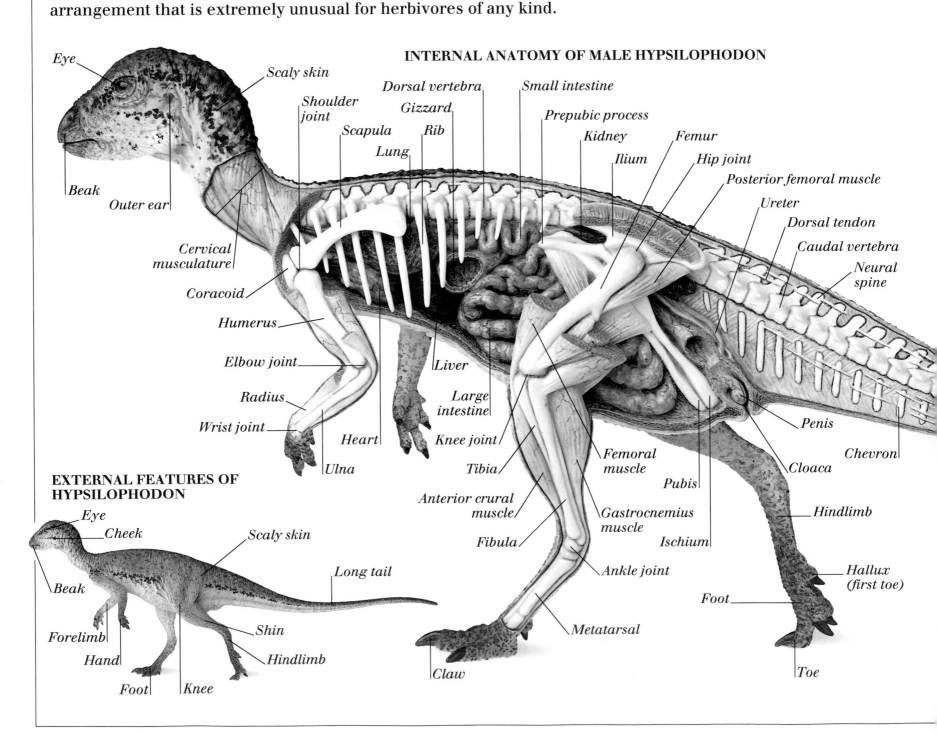

EXTERNAL FEATURES OF HYPSILOPHODON

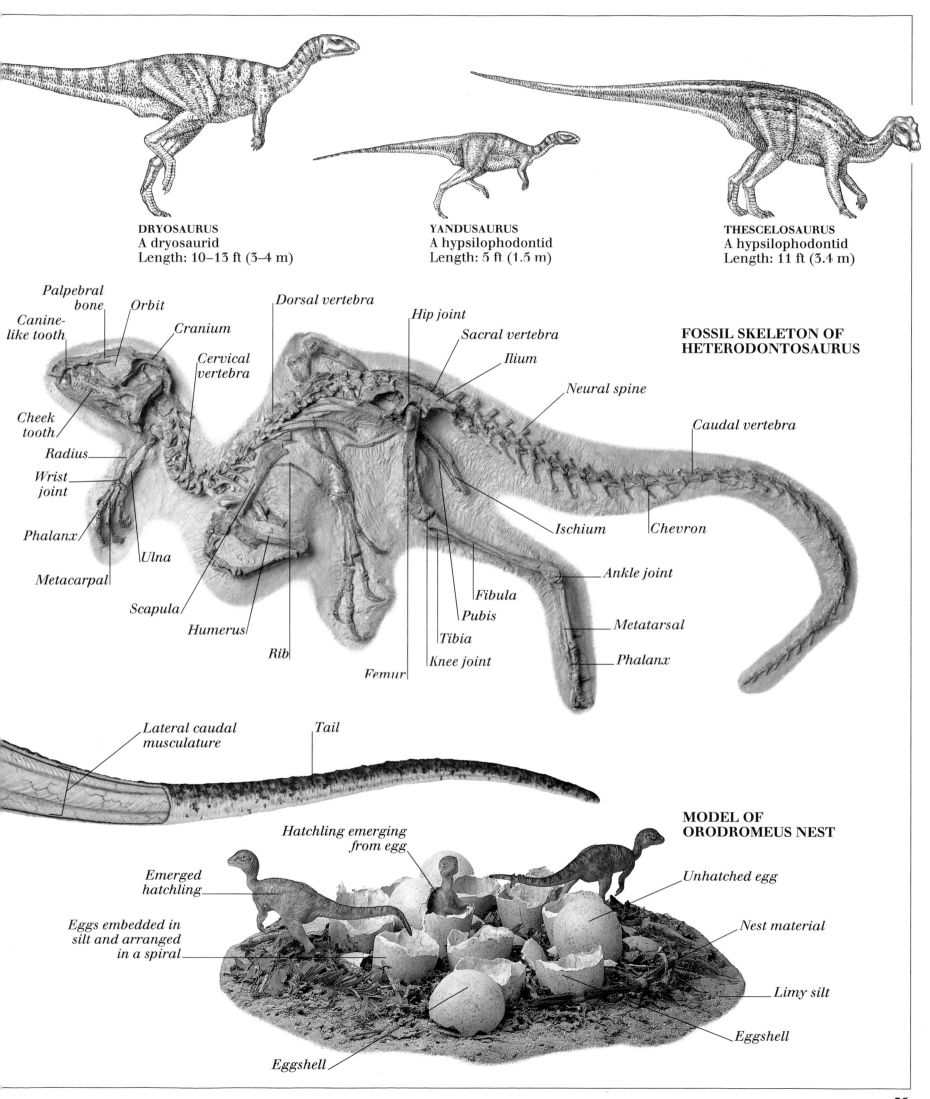

DRYOSAURUS
A dryosaurid
Length: 10–13 ft (3–4 m)

YANDUSAURUS
A hypsilophodontid
Length: 5 ft (1.5 m)

THESCELOSAURUS
A hypsilophodontid
Length: 11 ft (3.4 m)

FOSSIL SKELETON OF HETERODONTOSAURUS

Palpebral bone
Orbit
Canine-like tooth
Cranium
Cheek tooth
Cervical vertebra
Dorsal vertebra
Hip joint
Sacral vertebra
Ilium
Neural spine
Caudal vertebra
Radius
Wrist joint
Phalanx
Metacarpal
Ulna
Scapula
Humerus
Rib
Femur
Knee joint
Tibia
Pubis
Fibula
Ischium
Chevron
Ankle joint
Metatarsal
Phalanx

Lateral caudal musculature
Tail

MODEL OF ORODROMEUS NEST

Hatchling emerging from egg
Emerged hatchling
Unhatched egg
Eggs embedded in silt and arranged in a spiral
Nest material
Limy silt
Eggshell
Eggshell

35

Iguanodonts

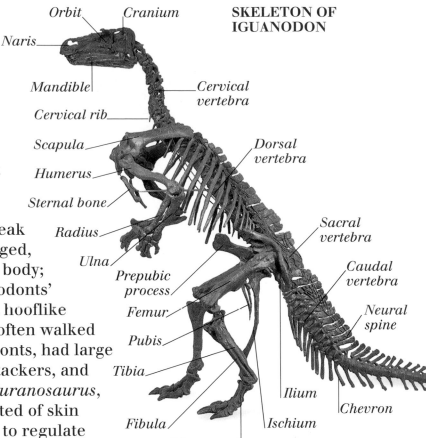

SKELETON OF IGUANODON

Orbit
Cranium
Naris
Mandible
Cervical vertebra
Cervical rib
Scapula
Dorsal vertebra
Humerus
Sternal bone
Radius
Sacral vertebra
Ulna
Prepubic process
Caudal vertebra
Femur
Neural spine
Pubis
Tibia
Ilium
Chevron
Fibula
Ischium
Metatarsal

IGUANODONTS WERE A GROUP of herbivorous (plant-eating), ornithischian (bird-hipped) dinosaurs that lived from Late Jurassic to Late Cretaceous times (165–70 million years ago). They were medium- to large-size dinosaurs – between 11 ft 6 in (3.5 m) and 33 ft (10 m) long – and lived in what are now North America, Europe, Africa, Asia, and Australia. Typically, iguanodonts had a broad, toothless beak at the end of a long snout; large jaws with long rows of ridged, close-packed cheek teeth, for grinding vegetation; a bulky body; and a heavy tail that was stiffened by bony tendons. Iguanodonts' powerful hindlimbs enabled them to run from danger, but hooflike nails on their fingers and toes indicate that they probably often walked on all fours. *Iguanodon*, and probably some other iguanodonts, had large thumb spikes that were probably strong enough to stab attackers, and flexible little fingers. The most unusual iguanodont was *Ouranosaurus*, which had a "sail" along its back. The sail probably consisted of skin stretched tightly over upright spines and may have served to regulate body temperature by absorbing and radiating heat. Some authorities believe that all iguanodonts belong to one group, the iguanodontids. However, others divide them into two subgroups: iguanodontids, such as *Iguanodon*, *Ouranosaurus*, and *Probactrosaurus*, and camptosaurids, such as *Camptosaurus* and possibly *Muttaburrasaurus*. This division is based on the number of toes of the dinosaurs: iguanodontids had three toes, while camptosaurids had four.

IGUANODON TOOTH

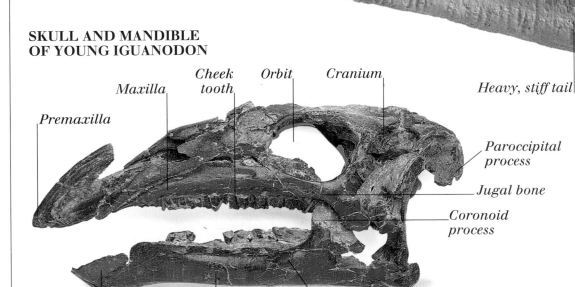

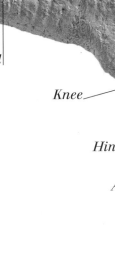

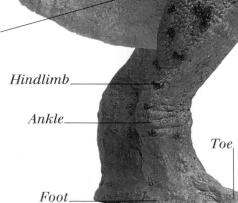

Thigh
Heavy, stiff tail
Knee
Hindlimb
Ankle
Toe
Foot
Hooflike nail

SKULL AND MANDIBLE OF YOUNG IGUANODON

Cheek tooth
Orbit
Cranium
Maxilla
Premaxilla
Paroccipital process
Jugal bone
Coronoid process
Predentary bone
Dentary bone
Mandible

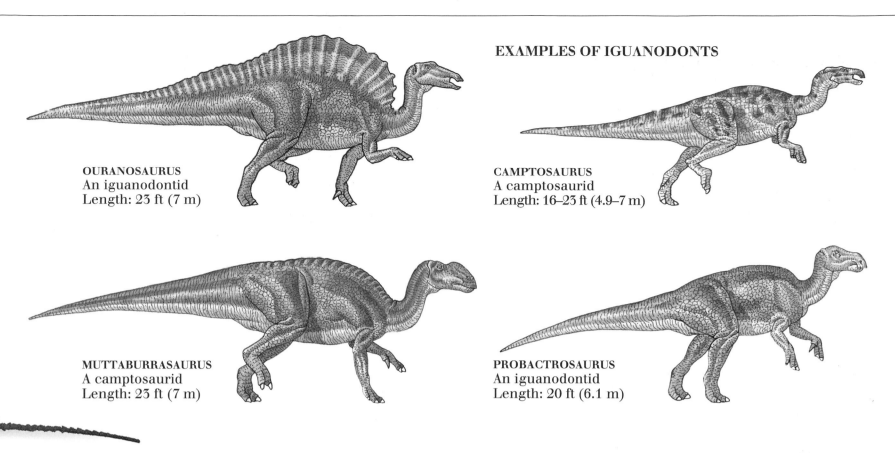

EXAMPLES OF IGUANODONTS

OURANOSAURUS
An iguanodontid
Length: 23 ft (7 m)

CAMPTOSAURUS
A camptosaurid
Length: 16–23 ft (4.9–7 m)

MUTTABURRASAURUS
A camptosaurid
Length: 23 ft (7 m)

PROBACTROSAURUS
An iguanodontid
Length: 20 ft (6.1 m)

EXTERNAL FEATURES OF IGUANODON

INTERNAL ANATOMY OF HIND LEG OF IGUANODON

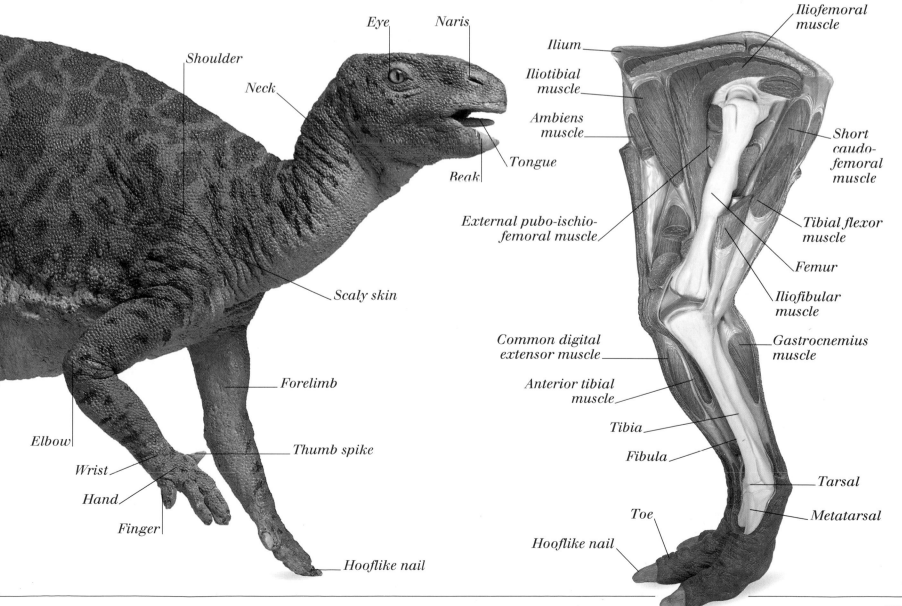

External features of Iguanodon labels: Eye, Naris, Shoulder, Neck, Tongue, Beak, Scaly skin, Forelimb, Thumb spike, Elbow, Wrist, Hand, Finger, Hooflike nail

Internal anatomy of hind leg labels: Iliofemoral muscle, Ilium, Iliotibial muscle, Ambiens muscle, External pubo-ischio-femoral muscle, Short caudo-femoral muscle, Tibial flexor muscle, Femur, Iliofibular muscle, Common digital extensor muscle, Gastrocnemius muscle, Anterior tibial muscle, Tibia, Fibula, Tarsal, Metatarsal, Toe, Hooflike nail

37

Hadrosaurs 1

FOSSIL SKELETON OF YOUNG HADROSAUR

HADROSAURS WERE a group of ornithischian (bird-hipped) dinosaurs that lived during Late Cretaceous times (97.5–65 million years ago) in what are now North America, Asia, and Europe. A characteristic feature of these herbivorous (plant-eating) dinosaurs was a beak similar to a duck's bill, which is the reason why hadrosaurs are sometimes known as duckbills. Although the beak was toothless, hadrosaurs had large numbers of cheek teeth – sometimes more than 300 in each jaw – for grinding tough vegetation. Hadrosaurs ranged from 13 ft (4 m) to 49 ft (14.9 m) in length. They walked on all fours but ran on their hind limbs, balancing their heavy bodies with a long, stiffened tail. There were two main subgroups of hadrosaurs: hadrosaurines, such as *Gryposaurus* and *Maiasaura*, and lambeosaurines, such as *Corythosaurus* and *Parasaurolophus*. The main difference between the subgroups was the shape of the skull. Hadrosaurines had flat skulls, some with bumps of solid bone on the snout, while the skulls of lambeosaurines had large, hollow, bony crests.

SKELETON OF YOUNG MAIASAURA

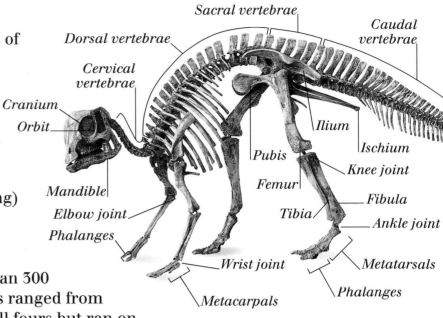

Sacral vertebrae
Dorsal vertebrae
Caudal vertebrae
Cervical vertebrae
Cranium
Orbit
Ilium
Ischium
Pubis
Knee joint
Femur
Mandible
Fibula
Elbow joint
Tibia
Ankle joint
Phalanges
Metatarsals
Wrist joint
Phalanges
Metacarpals

FOSSIL SKELETON OF GRYPOSAURUS

Caudal vertebrae (end vertebrae missing)

Neural spine
Chevron
Ossified tendon
Ischium

MODEL OF MAIASAURA NEST

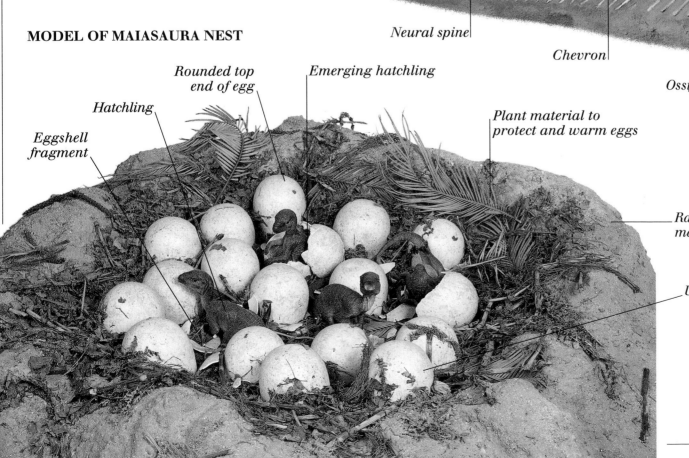

Rounded top end of egg
Emerging hatchling
Hatchling
Eggshell fragment
Plant material to protect and warm eggs
Raised nest made of sand
Unhatched egg
Ankle joint

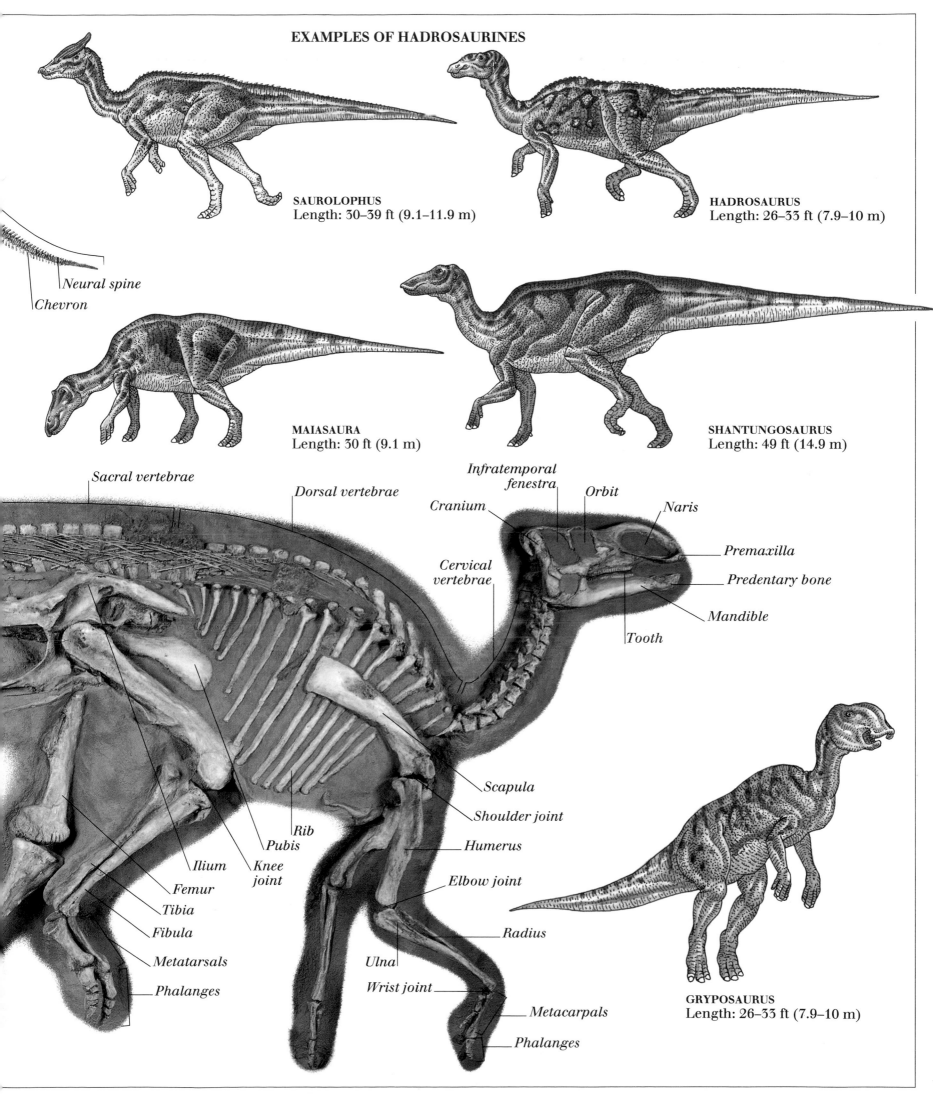

EXAMPLES OF HADROSAURINES

SAUROLOPHUS
Length: 30–39 ft (9.1–11.9 m)

HADROSAURUS
Length: 26–33 ft (7.9–10 m)

Neural spine

Chevron

MAIASAURA
Length: 30 ft (9.1 m)

SHANTUNGOSAURUS
Length: 49 ft (14.9 m)

Sacral vertebrae

Dorsal vertebrae

Infratemporal fenestra

Cranium

Orbit

Naris

Cervical vertebrae

Premaxilla

Predentary bone

Mandible

Tooth

Scapula

Shoulder joint

Humerus

Rib

Pubis

Elbow joint

Ilium

Knee joint

Femur

Radius

Tibia

Ulna

Fibula

Metatarsals

Wrist joint

Phalanges

Metacarpals

Phalanges

GRYPOSAURUS
Length: 26–33 ft (7.9–10 m)

Hadrosaurs 2

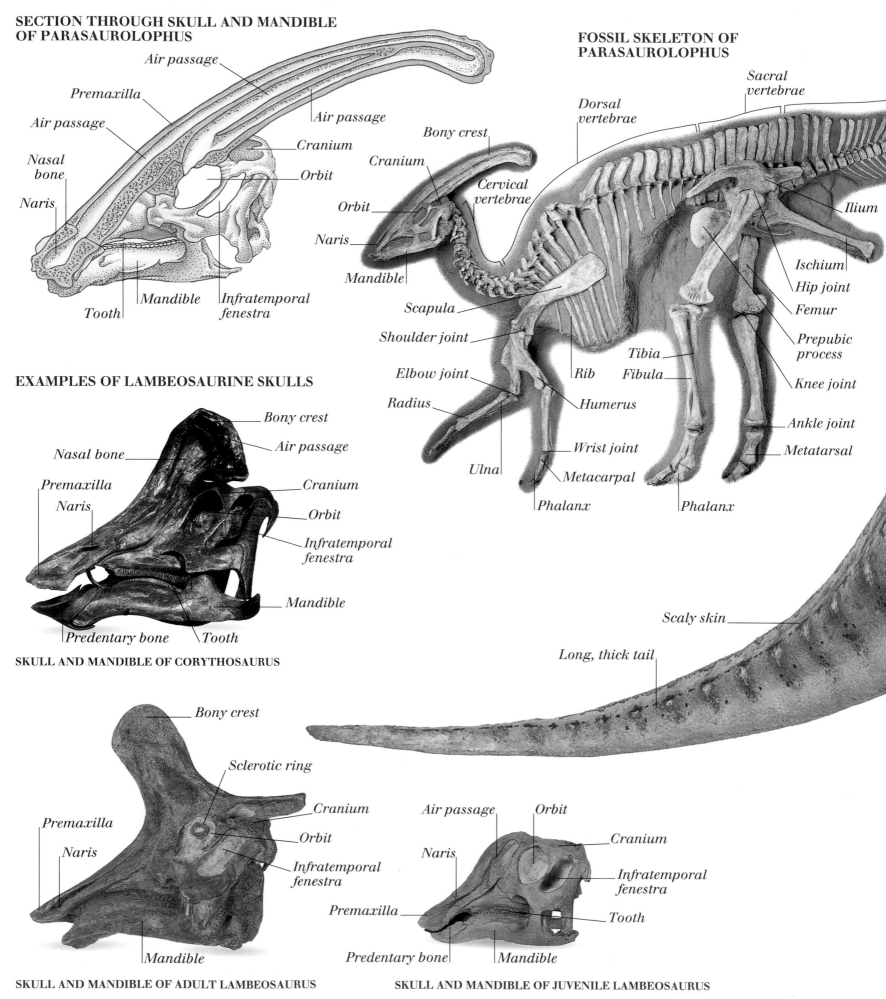

SECTION THROUGH SKULL AND MANDIBLE OF PARASAUROLOPHUS

Air passage

Premaxilla

Air passage

Air passage

Nasal bone

Cranium

Naris

Orbit

Tooth

Mandible

Infratemporal fenestra

FOSSIL SKELETON OF PARASAUROLOPHUS

Sacral vertebrae

Dorsal vertebrae

Bony crest

Cranium

Cervical vertebrae

Orbit

Ilium

Naris

Mandible

Ischium

Hip joint

Scapula

Femur

Shoulder joint

Prepubic process

Elbow joint

Tibia

Rib

Fibula

Knee joint

Radius

Humerus

Ulna

Wrist joint

Ankle joint

Metacarpal

Metatarsal

Phalanx

Phalanx

EXAMPLES OF LAMBEOSAURINE SKULLS

Bony crest

Nasal bone

Air passage

Premaxilla

Naris

Cranium

Orbit

Infratemporal fenestra

Mandible

Predentary bone

Tooth

SKULL AND MANDIBLE OF CORYTHOSAURUS

Scaly skin

Long, thick tail

Bony crest

Sclerotic ring

Premaxilla

Cranium

Naris

Orbit

Infratemporal fenestra

Mandible

SKULL AND MANDIBLE OF ADULT LAMBEOSAURUS

Air passage

Orbit

Naris

Cranium

Infratemporal fenestra

Premaxilla

Tooth

Predentary bone

Mandible

SKULL AND MANDIBLE OF JUVENILE LAMBEOSAURUS

EXTERNAL FEATURES OF CORYTHOSAURUS

Caudal vertebrae

Neural spine

Chevron

Bony crest

Eye

Naris

Toothless beak

Cheek pouch

Tongue

Neck

Shoulder

Forelimb

Elbow

Wrist

Hand

Finger

Nail

Knee

Thigh

Tubercle

Hindlimb

Ankle

Foot

Toe

Nail

EXAMPLES OF LAMBEOSAURINES

CORYTHOSAURUS
Length: 33 ft (10 m)

PARASAUROLOPHUS
Length: 33 ft (10 m)

HYPACROSAURUS
Length: 30 ft (9.1 m)

LAMBEOSAURUS
Length: 49 ft (14.9 m)

Stegosaurs

STEGOSAURS WERE A GROUP of ornithischian (bird-hipped) dinosaurs that lived from Middle Jurassic to Early Cretaceous times (188–97.5 million years ago) in what are now North America, Europe, Africa, and Asia. They were medium-size dinosaurs – between about 10 ft (3 m) and 30 ft (9.1 m) long – with bulky bodies that weighed up to about 1.5 tons. The main characteristic of stegosaurs was the two rows of dorsal plates or spines that ran along their backs. The exact function of these plates or spikes is not known, but it is thought that they may have been for defense, for display, or for regulating body temperature by absorbing or radiating heat. Also, probably for defense, stegosaurs had caudal (tail) spikes and, in some species, shoulder spikes. There were two main subgroups of stegosaurs: stegosaurids, such as *Stegosaurus*, *Tuojiangosaurus*, *Kentrosaurus*, and *Wuerhosaurus*, and huayangosaurids. *Huayangosaurus*, the only known huayangosaurid, resembled stegosaurids but is thought to have been more primitive.

EXAMPLES OF STEGOSAURS

WUERHOSAURUS
A stegosaurid
Length: 20 ft (6.1 m)

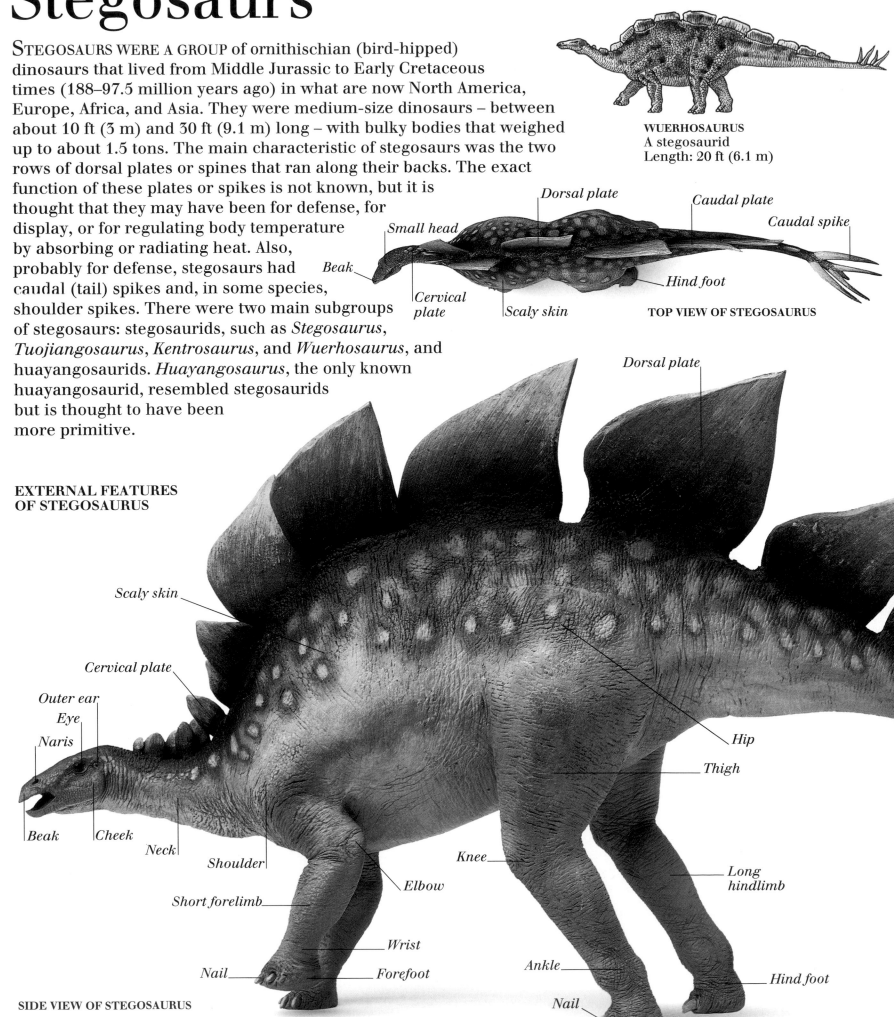

Dorsal plate

Caudal plate

Caudal spike

Small head

Beak

Hind foot

Cervical plate

Scaly skin

TOP VIEW OF STEGOSAURUS

Dorsal plate

EXTERNAL FEATURES OF STEGOSAURUS

Scaly skin

Cervical plate

Outer ear

Eye

Naris

Hip

Thigh

Beak

Cheek

Neck

Shoulder

Knee

Elbow

Long hindlimb

Short forelimb

Wrist

Nail

Forefoot

Ankle

Hind foot

Nail

SIDE VIEW OF STEGOSAURUS

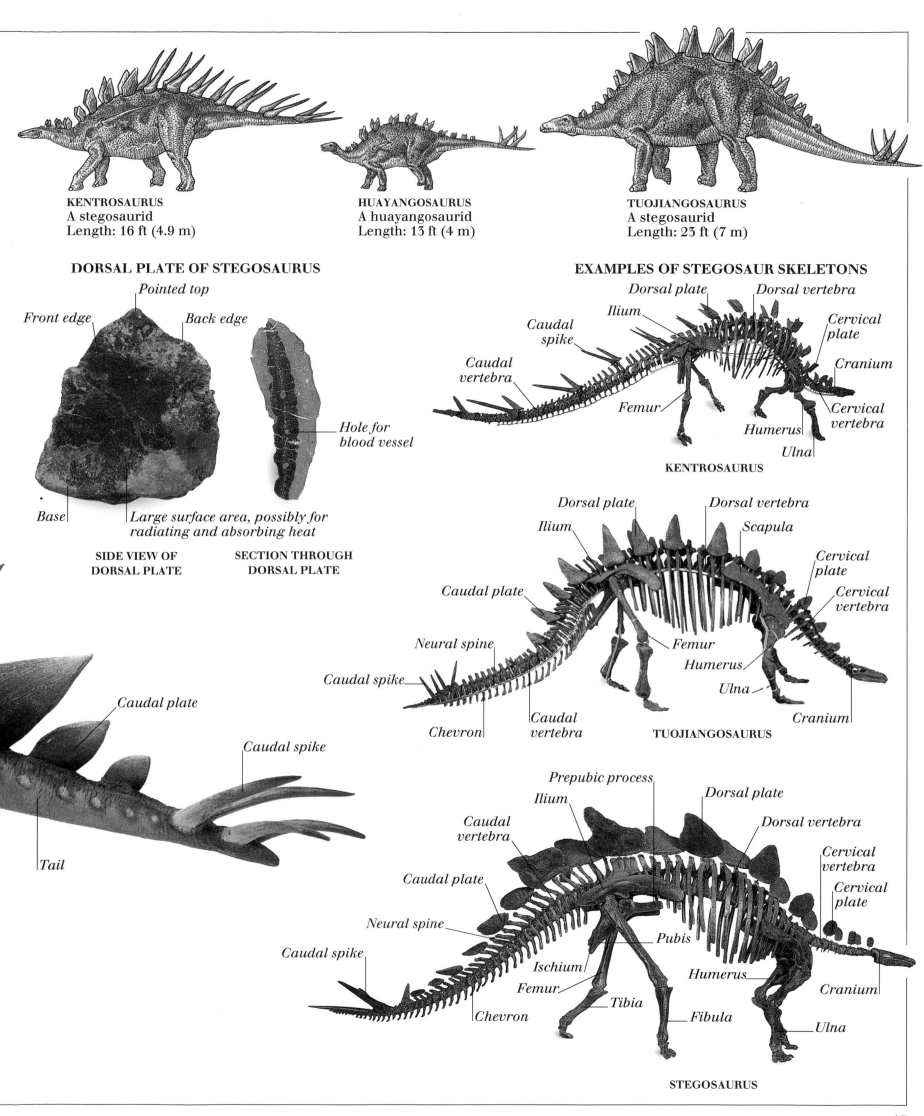

KENTROSAURUS
A stegosaurid
Length: 16 ft (4.9 m)

HUAYANGOSAURUS
A huayangosaurid
Length: 13 ft (4 m)

TUOJIANGOSAURUS
A stegosaurid
Length: 23 ft (7 m)

DORSAL PLATE OF STEGOSAURUS

Pointed top

Front edge

Back edge

Hole for blood vessel

Base

Large surface area, possibly for radiating and absorbing heat

SIDE VIEW OF DORSAL PLATE

SECTION THROUGH DORSAL PLATE

EXAMPLES OF STEGOSAUR SKELETONS

Dorsal plate

Dorsal vertebra

Ilium

Caudal spike

Cervical plate

Caudal vertebra

Cranium

Femur

Cervical vertebra

Humerus

Ulna

KENTROSAURUS

Dorsal plate

Dorsal vertebra

Ilium

Scapula

Cervical plate

Caudal plate

Cervical vertebra

Neural spine

Femur

Humerus

Caudal spike

Ulna

Chevron

Caudal vertebra

Cranium

TUOJIANGOSAURUS

Caudal plate

Caudal spike

Tail

Prepubic process

Dorsal plate

Ilium

Dorsal vertebra

Caudal vertebra

Cervical vertebra

Caudal plate

Cervical plate

Neural spine

Pubis

Ischium

Humerus

Caudal spike

Femur

Cranium

Tibia

Fibula

Chevron

Ulna

STEGOSAURUS

Ankylosaurs

ANKYLOSAURS WERE A GROUP OF HERBIVOROUS (plant-eating), ornithischian (bird-hipped) dinosaurs that lived from Middle Jurassic to Late Cretaceous times (188–65 million years ago) in what are now Mongolia, North America, Antarctica, Australia, and Europe. They ranged from 8 ft (2.4 m) to 35 ft (10.7 m) long, and weighed up to 2 tons. The most notable feature of these dinosaurs was their heavy armor, which consisted of bony studs, plates, and spikes that protected them from predators. Ankylosaurs also had characteristics typical of herbivorous dinosaurs: toothless beaks and cheek teeth, for cropping and chewing vegetation. It is possible that ankylosaurs also had a gizzard (muscular stomach) and gastroliths (stones) for further breaking down plant material in the gut. There were two main subgroups of ankylosaurs: ankylosaurids, such as *Ankylosaurus*, *Euoplocephalus*, and *Pinacosaurus*; and nodosaurids, such as *Edmontonia*, *Minmi*, *Panoplosaurus*, and *Polacanthus*. The most apparent differences between the subgroups were that ankylosaurids had horns on their head and a bony tail club, while nodosaurids tended to have neither.

SHOULDER SPIKE OF POLACANTHUS

EXAMPLES OF ANKYLOSAURS

MINMI
A nodosaurid
Length: 8 ft (2.4 m)

FOSSIL OF ANKYLOSAURUS TAIL CLUB

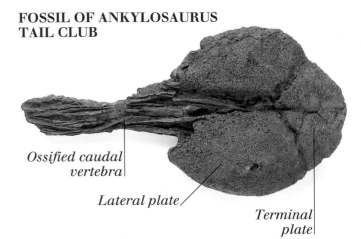

Ossified caudal vertebra

Lateral plate

Terminal plate

INTERNAL ANATOMY OF FEMALE EUOPLOCEPHALUS

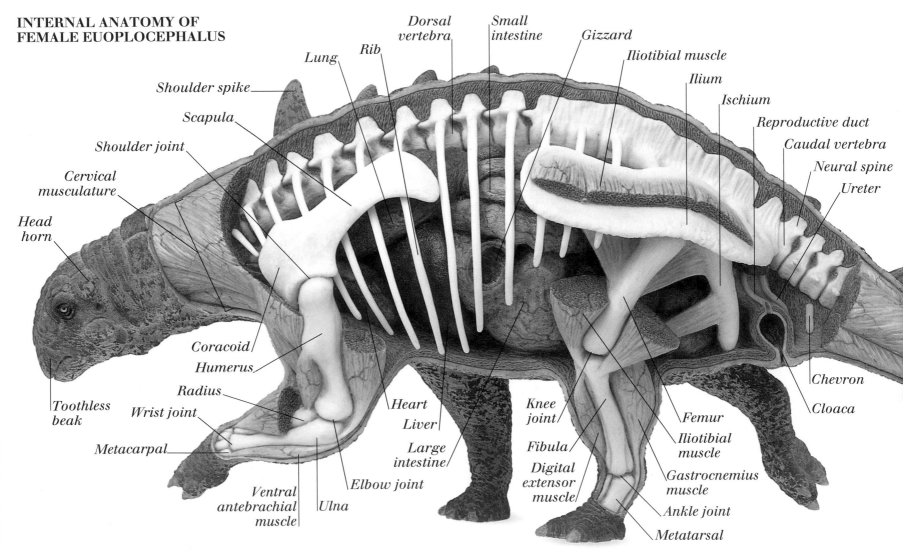

Dorsal vertebra

Small intestine

Gizzard

Iliotibial muscle

Ilium

Ischium

Reproductive duct

Caudal vertebra

Neural spine

Ureter

Lung

Rib

Shoulder spike

Scapula

Shoulder joint

Cervical musculature

Head horn

Coracoid

Humerus

Radius

Wrist joint

Metacarpal

Toothless beak

Ventral antebrachial muscle

Ulna

Elbow joint

Heart

Liver

Large intestine

Knee joint

Fibula

Digital extensor muscle

Femur

Iliotibial muscle

Gastrocnemius muscle

Ankle joint

Metatarsal

Chevron

Cloaca

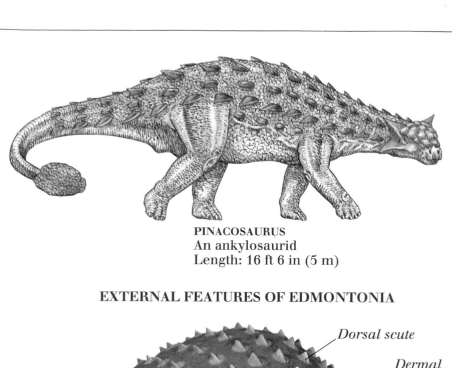

PINACOSAURUS
An ankylosaurid
Length: 16 ft 6 in (5 m)

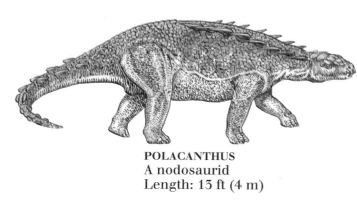

POLACANTHUS
A nodosaurid
Length: 13 ft (4 m)

EXTERNAL FEATURES OF EDMONTONIA

Dorsal scute

Dermal armor

Scaly skin

Hindlimb

Flank spike

Nuchal ring

Knee

Shoulder spike

Armored tail

Ankle

Hindfoot

Elbow

Forelimb

Forefoot

Eye

Blunt nail

Naris

Broad, flat snout

Lateral caudal musculature

Tail club

EXAMPLES OF ANKYLOSAUR SKULLS

Orbit

Cranium

Nasal bone

Maxilla

Naris

Beak

Infratemporal fenestra

Mandible

SKULL AND MANDIBLE OF PANOPLOSAURUS

Posterolateral horn

Orbit

Cranium

Maxilla

Naris

Beak

Tooth

Jugal plate

Mandible

SKULL AND MANDIBLE OF EUOPLOCEPHALUS

Posterolateral horn

Orbit

Cranium

Nasal bone

Naris

Beak

Maxilla

Tooth

Mandible

Jugal plate

SKULL AND MANDIBLE OF ANKYLOSAURUS

45

Pachycephalosaurs

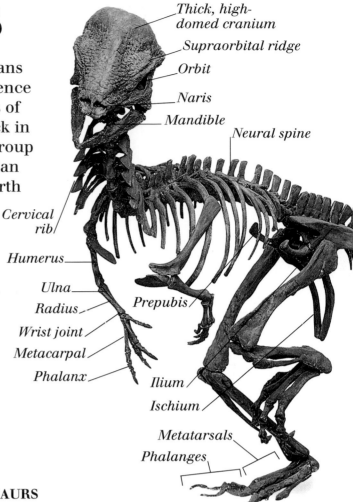

THE TERM "pachycephalosaur" means "thick-headed lizard," a reference to the extremely thick-roofed skulls of these dinosaurs – up to 10 in (25 cm) thick in some cases. Pachycephalosaurs were a group of herbivorous (plant-eating), ornithischian (bird-hipped) dinosaurs that lived predominantly in what are now North America, Madagascar, China, and Mongolia in Late Cretaceous times (97.5–65 million years ago). Their thick skulls were probably designed to protect their brains during head-butting contests to win territory and mates; their hips and spine were also strengthened to withstand the shock of head-butting. Pachycephalosaurs ranged from about 20 in (50 cm) to 15 ft (4.6 m) in length. They had short arms, long, stiff tails to aid balance, and thickset bodies. There were two main subgroups of pachycephalosaurs: pachycephalosaurids, such as *Pachycephalosaurus, Stegoceras,* and *Prenocephale,* and homalocephalids, such as *Homalocephale* and *Wannanosaurus.* Pachycephalosaurids had thick, high-domed skulls that could withstand heavier blows than the less thick, flat-topped skulls of homalocephalids.

HEAD-BUTTING PRENOCEPHALES

Thick, high-domed cranium
Supraorbital ridge
Orbit
Naris
Mandible
Neural spine
Cervical rib
Humerus
Ulna
Radius
Prepubis
Wrist joint
Metacarpal
Phalanx
Ilium
Ischium
Metatarsals
Phalanges

EXAMPLES OF SKULLS OF PACHYCEPHALOSAURS

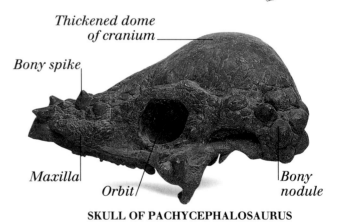

Orbit
Thickened dome of cranium
Maxilla
Bony ridge
Tooth
Mandible

SKULL AND MANDIBLE OF STEGOCERAS

Thickened dome of cranium
Orbit
Maxilla
Bony nodule

SKULL OF PRENOCEPHALE

Thickened dome of cranium
Bony spike
Maxilla
Orbit
Bony nodule

SKULL OF PACHYCEPHALOSAURUS

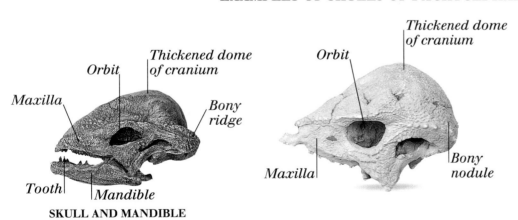

EXTERNAL FEATURES OF PACHYCEPHALOSAURUS

Bony nodule
Scaly skin
Domed head
Eye
Bony spike
Neck
Snout
Tail
Knee
Forelimb
Hindlimb
Finger
Ankle
Hand
Claw
Foot
Toe

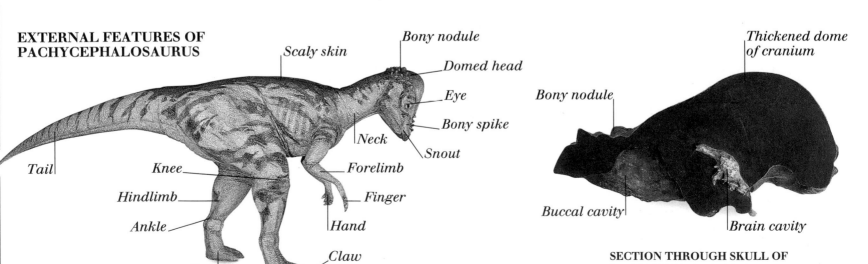

Thickened dome of cranium
Bony nodule
Buccal cavity
Brain cavity

SECTION THROUGH SKULL OF PACHYCEPHALOSAURUS

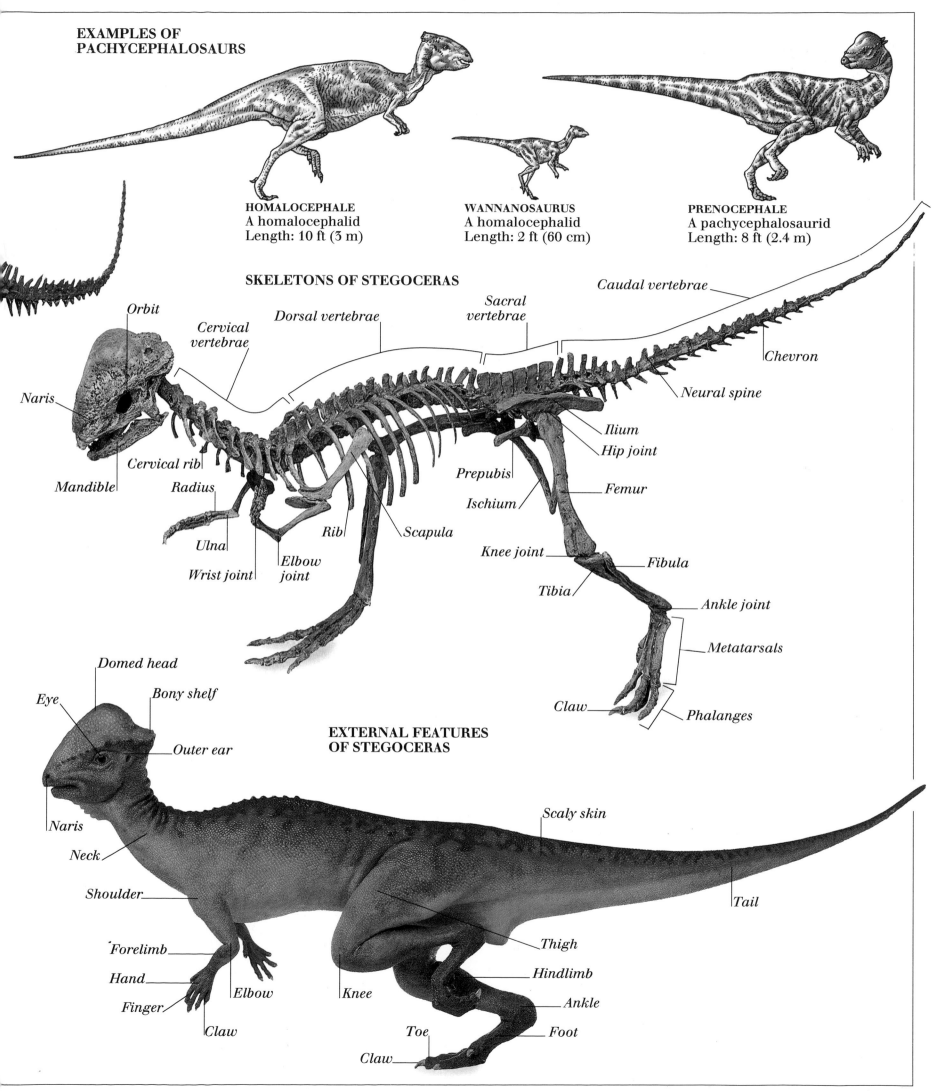

EXAMPLES OF PACHYCEPHALOSAURS

HOMALOCEPHALE
A homalocephalid
Length: 10 ft (3 m)

WANNANOSAURUS
A homalocephalid
Length: 2 ft (60 cm)

PRENOCEPHALE
A pachycephalosaurid
Length: 8 ft (2.4 m)

SKELETONS OF STEGOCERAS

Caudal vertebrae

Sacral
vertebrae

Dorsal vertebrae

Orbit

Cervical
vertebrae

Chevron

Naris

Neural spine

Ilium

Cervical rib

Hip joint

Mandible

Prepubis

Radius

Femur

Ischium

Rib

Scapula

Ulna

Wrist joint

Elbow
joint

Knee joint

Fibula

Tibia

Ankle joint

Metatarsals

Claw

Phalanges

EXTERNAL FEATURES
OF STEGOCERAS

Domed head

Bony shelf

Eye

Outer ear

Naris

Scaly skin

Neck

Shoulder

Tail

Forelimb

Thigh

Hand

Hindlimb

Knee

Finger

Ankle

Elbow

Claw

Toe

Foot

Claw

Ceratopsians 1

NEST AND EGGS OF PROTOCERATOPS

CERATOPSIANS WERE A GROUP of ornithischian (bird-hipped), herbivorous (plant-eating) dinosaurs with short, deep, parrot-like beaks. These dinosaurs flourished during the Cretaceous period (144–65 million years ago). There were three subgroups of ceratopsians: protoceratopsids, ceratopsids, and psittacosaurids. Protoceratopsids, such as *Protoceratops*, *Bagaceratops*, and *Microceratops*, were relatively small, ranging from 30 in (76 cm) to 10 ft (3 m) long. They had a bony frill around the neck that may have been used to frighten predators, protect the neck, or attract mates; the frill may also have served as an anchor for the jaw muscles. Some species of protoceratopsid also had brow ridges and small horns on their noses and cheeks. Ceratopsids, such as *Triceratops*, *Torosaurus*, *Styracosaurus*, *Pachyrhinosaurus*, and *Eucentrosaurus*, were larger than protoceratopsids, ranging from 6 ft (1.8 m) to 30 ft (9.1 m) in length. *Triceratops*, one of the largest ceratopsids, had a massive head and bulky body, and weighed up to about 5.4 tons. Ceratopsids had neck frills that were larger than those of protoceratopsids, and horns on their brow and nose. In some cases, ceratopsid brow horns were up to 3 ft (90 cm) long. *Psittacosaurus*, the only psittacosaurid known, was 6 ft 6 in (2 m) long. In addition to the parrot-like ceratopsian beak, it had small cheek horns; however, it did not have a bony neck frill.

SECTION THROUGH CERATOPSIAN EGG

- Yolk sac
- Embryo
- Amniotic sac
- Allantois
- Chorion
- Shell

SKULL AND MANDIBLE OF PROTOCERATOPS

- Parietosquamosal frill
- Cranium
- Postorbital bone
- Orbit
- Nasal bone
- Lacrimal bone
- Naris
- Beak
- Rostral bone
- Predentary bone
- Dentary bone
- Tooth
- Parietal fenestra
- Infratemporal fenestra
- Jugal bone
- Surangular bone
- Angular bone
- Mandible
- Tail

FOSSIL SKELETON OF PROTOCERATOPS

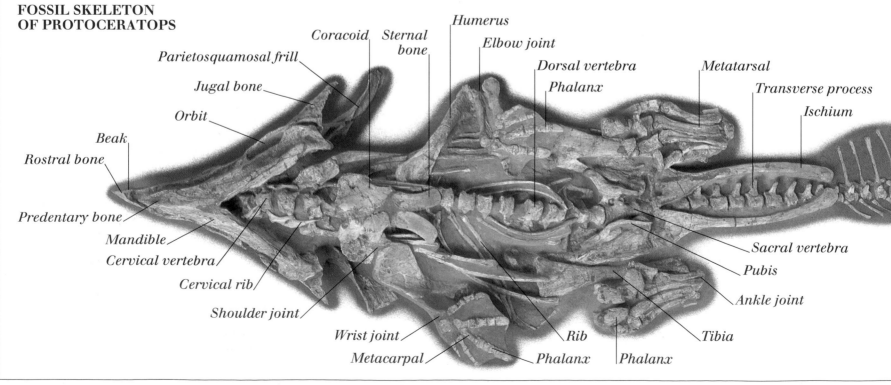

- Parietosquamosal frill
- Jugal bone
- Orbit
- Beak
- Rostral bone
- Predentary bone
- Mandible
- Cervical vertebra
- Cervical rib
- Shoulder joint
- Wrist joint
- Metacarpal
- Coracoid
- Sternal bone
- Humerus
- Elbow joint
- Dorsal vertebra
- Phalanx
- Phalanx
- Rib
- Phalanx
- Phalanx
- Tibia
- Metatarsal
- Transverse process
- Ischium
- Sacral vertebra
- Pubis
- Ankle joint

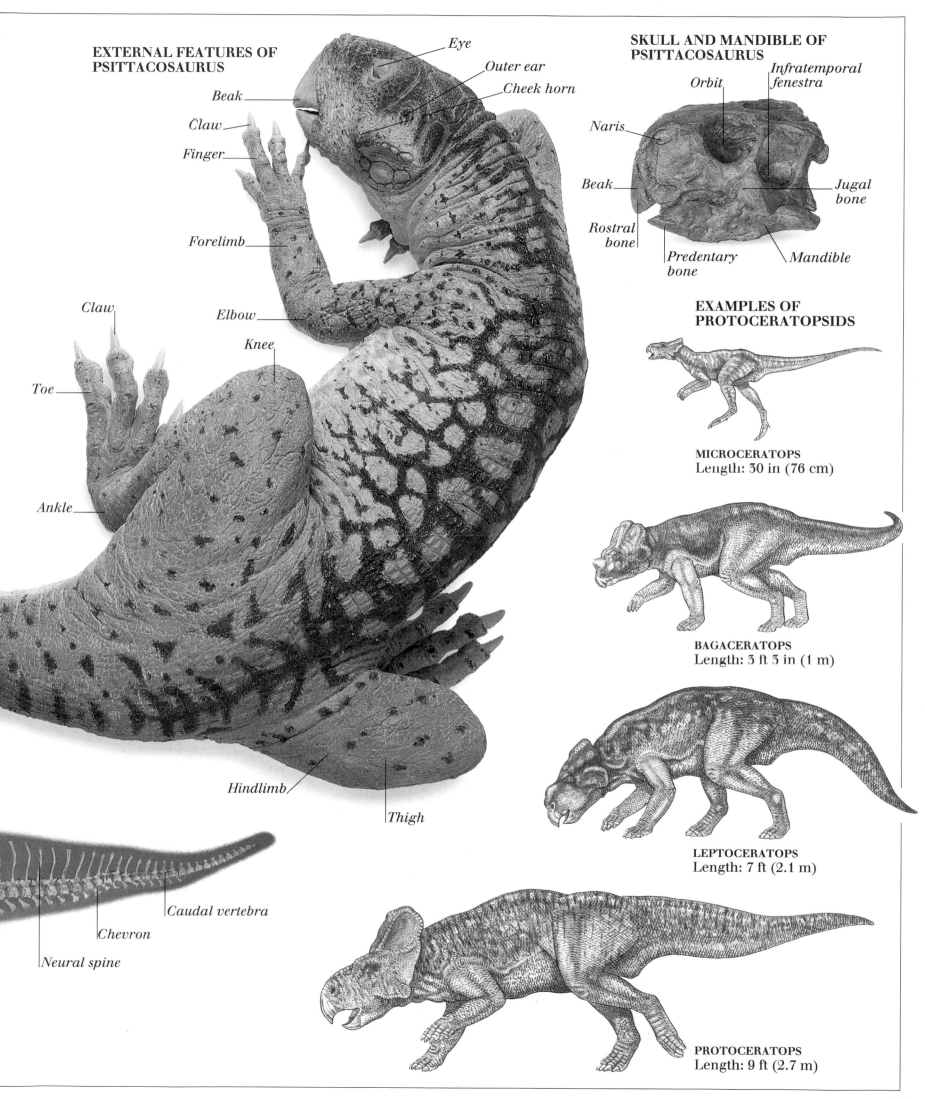

EXTERNAL FEATURES OF PSITTACOSAURUS

Eye

Beak

Claw

Finger

Outer ear

Cheek horn

Forelimb

Elbow

Knee

Claw

Toe

Ankle

Hindlimb

Thigh

Caudal vertebra

Chevron

Neural spine

SKULL AND MANDIBLE OF PSITTACOSAURUS

Orbit

Infratemporal fenestra

Naris

Beak

Jugal bone

Rostral bone

Predentary bone

Mandible

EXAMPLES OF PROTOCERATOPSIDS

MICROCERATOPS
Length: 30 in (76 cm)

BAGACERATOPS
Length: 3 ft 3 in (1 m)

LEPTOCERATOPS
Length: 7 ft (2.1 m)

PROTOCERATOPS
Length: 9 ft (2.7 m)

Ceratopsians 2

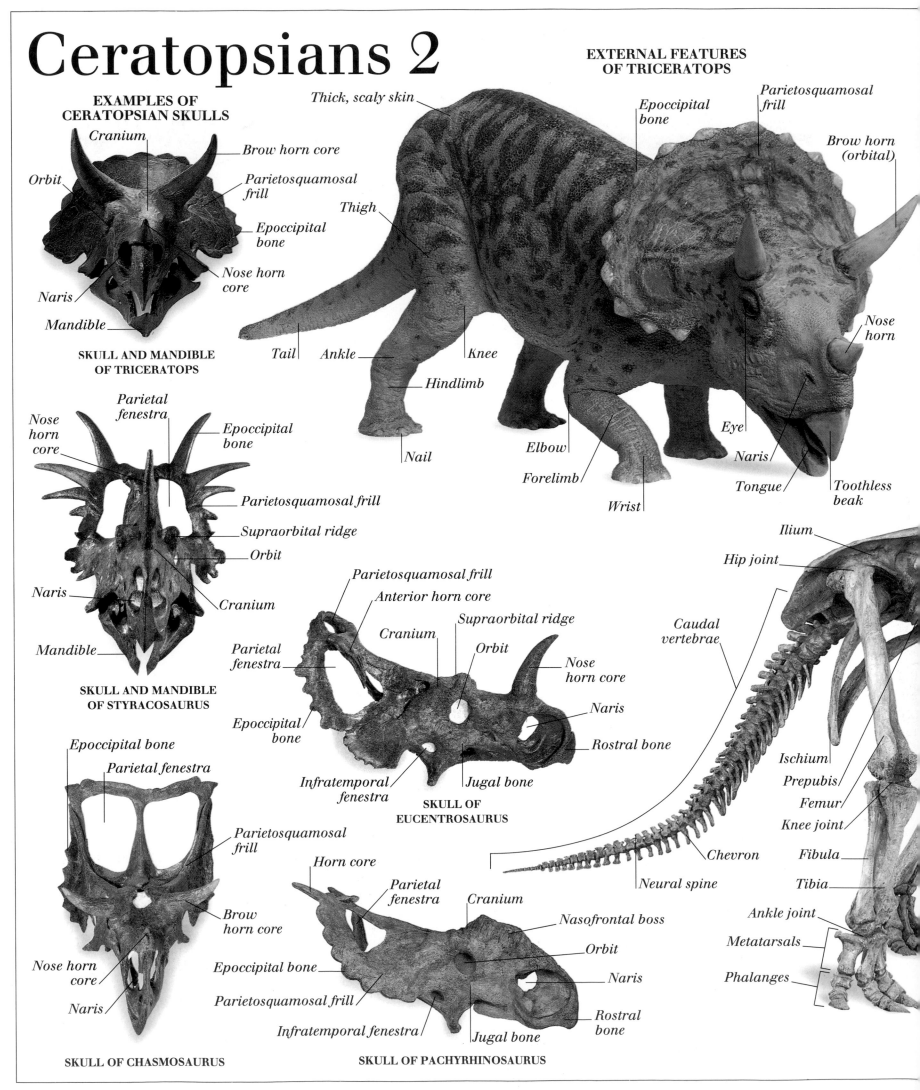

EXAMPLES OF CERATOPSIAN SKULLS

Cranium
Brow horn core
Orbit
Parietosquamosal frill
Epoccipital bone
Nose horn core
Naris
Mandible

SKULL AND MANDIBLE OF TRICERATOPS

Nose horn core
Parietal fenestra
Epoccipital bone
Parietosquamosal frill
Supraorbital ridge
Orbit
Naris
Cranium
Mandible

SKULL AND MANDIBLE OF STYRACOSAURUS

Epoccipital bone
Parietal fenestra
Parietosquamosal frill
Brow horn core
Nose horn core
Naris

SKULL OF CHASMOSAURUS

EXTERNAL FEATURES OF TRICERATOPS

Thick, scaly skin
Epoccipital bone
Parietosquamosal frill
Brow horn (orbital)
Thigh
Nose horn
Tail
Ankle
Knee
Hindlimb
Nail
Elbow
Eye
Naris
Forelimb
Tongue
Toothless beak
Wrist

Parietosquamosal frill
Anterior horn core
Cranium
Supraorbital ridge
Orbit
Parietal fenestra
Nose horn core
Naris
Epoccipital bone
Rostral bone
Infratemporal fenestra
Jugal bone

SKULL OF EUCENTROSAURUS

Horn core
Parietal fenestra
Cranium
Nasofrontal boss
Orbit
Epoccipital bone
Naris
Parietosquamosal frill
Rostral bone
Infratemporal fenestra
Jugal bone

SKULL OF PACHYRHINOSAURUS

Ilium
Hip joint
Caudal vertebrae
Ischium
Prepubis
Femur
Knee joint
Fibula
Chevron
Tibia
Neural spine
Ankle joint
Metatarsals
Phalanges

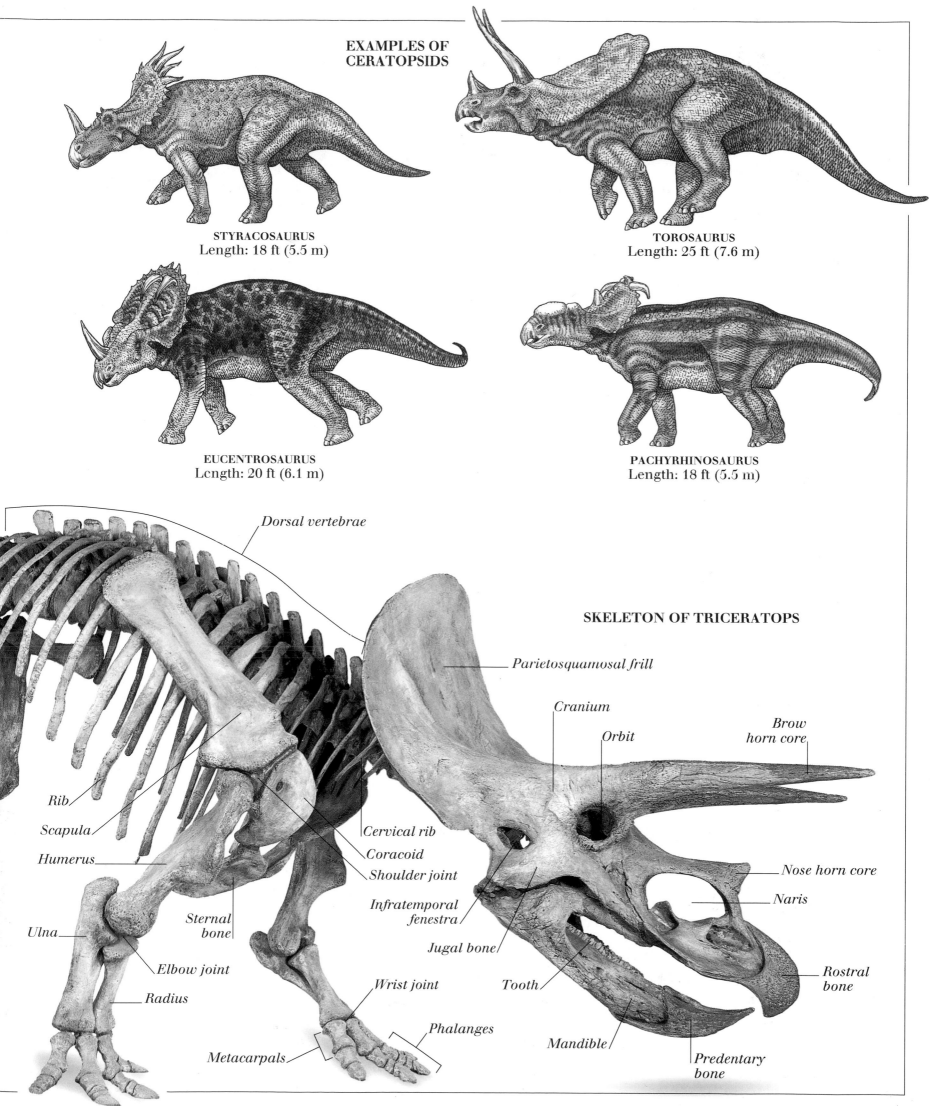

EXAMPLES OF CERATOPSIDS

STYRACOSAURUS
Length: 18 ft (5.5 m)

TOROSAURUS
Length: 25 ft (7.6 m)

EUCENTROSAURUS
Length: 20 ft (6.1 m)

PACHYRHINOSAURUS
Length: 18 ft (5.5 m)

SKELETON OF TRICERATOPS

Dorsal vertebrae

Parietosquamosal frill

Cranium

Orbit

Brow horn core

Rib

Scapula

Humerus

Cervical rib

Coracoid

Shoulder joint

Nose horn core

Naris

Ulna

Infratemporal fenestra

Sternal bone

Jugal bone

Elbow joint

Rostral bone

Radius

Wrist joint

Tooth

Phalanges

Metacarpals

Mandible

Predentary bone

Hands and claws

FOSSIL OF DINOSAUR CLAW

THE HANDS OF CARNIVOROUS (flesh-eating) dinosaurs – *Deinocheirus* and *Baryonyx*, for example – typically had three fingers (although a few had two), each tipped with a sharp claw. Many carnivorous dinosaurs also had opposable fingers that enabled them to grasp. They walked on their hind legs, leaving their arms and hands free to attack prey. However, the arms of some carnivores, notably *Tyrannosaurus*, were so short that they did not even reach their mouths. Most herbivores (plant-eaters) had padded hands with four or five fingers, tipped with claws or blunt nails. Many herbivores also had sharp thumb claws for digging or defense. Unlike carnivores, herbivores did not generally have opposable fingers. Although many herbivores – *Iguanodon* and *Prosaurolophus*, for example – had strong, weight-bearing forelimbs, such dinosaurs could also walk or run on their hind legs alone.

EXAMPLES OF DINOSAUR CLAWS

Top part of claw (sharp point missing)

Claw used for digging and defense

Base

MASSOSPONDYLUS THUMB CLAW

Top part of claw (sharp point missing)

Flattened surface

Claw used as a hook

Base

ORNITHOMIMUS FINGER CLAW

Hook shape

Sharp tip

Claw used for catching fish

Base

BARYONYX THUMB CLAW

Top part of claw (sharp point missing)

Claw used for digging and defense

Broad surface

Base

APATOSAURUS THUMB CLAW

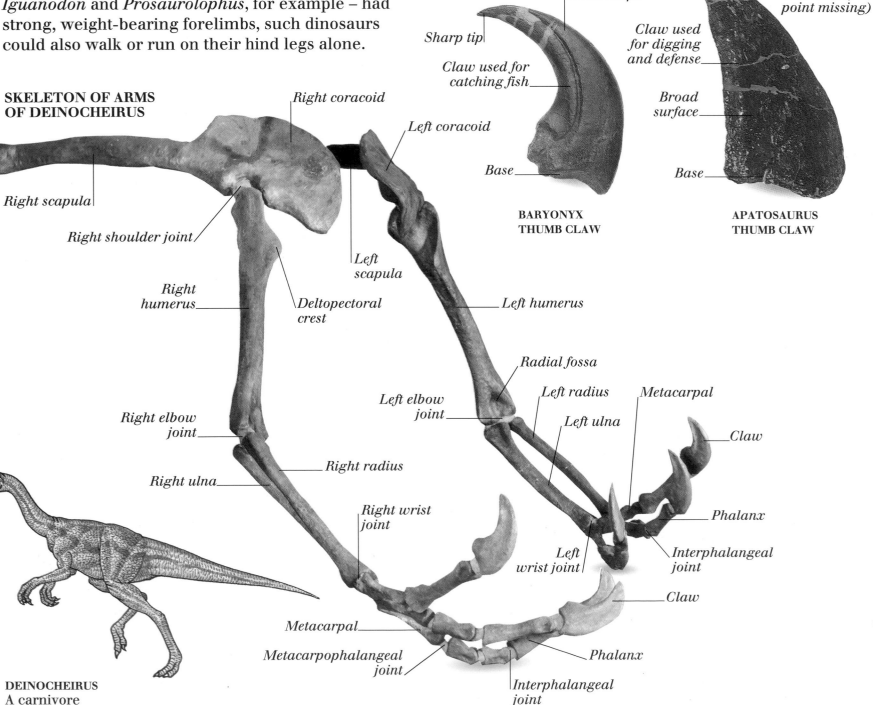

SKELETON OF ARMS OF DEINOCHEIRUS

Right coracoid

Left coracoid

Right scapula

Right shoulder joint

Left scapula

Right humerus

Deltopectoral crest

Left humerus

Radial fossa

Left elbow joint

Left radius

Metacarpal

Left ulna

Claw

Right elbow joint

Right radius

Right ulna

Phalanx

Right wrist joint

Interphalangeal joint

Left wrist joint

Claw

Metacarpal

Metacarpophalangeal joint

Phalanx

Interphalangeal joint

DEINOCHEIRUS
A carnivore

52

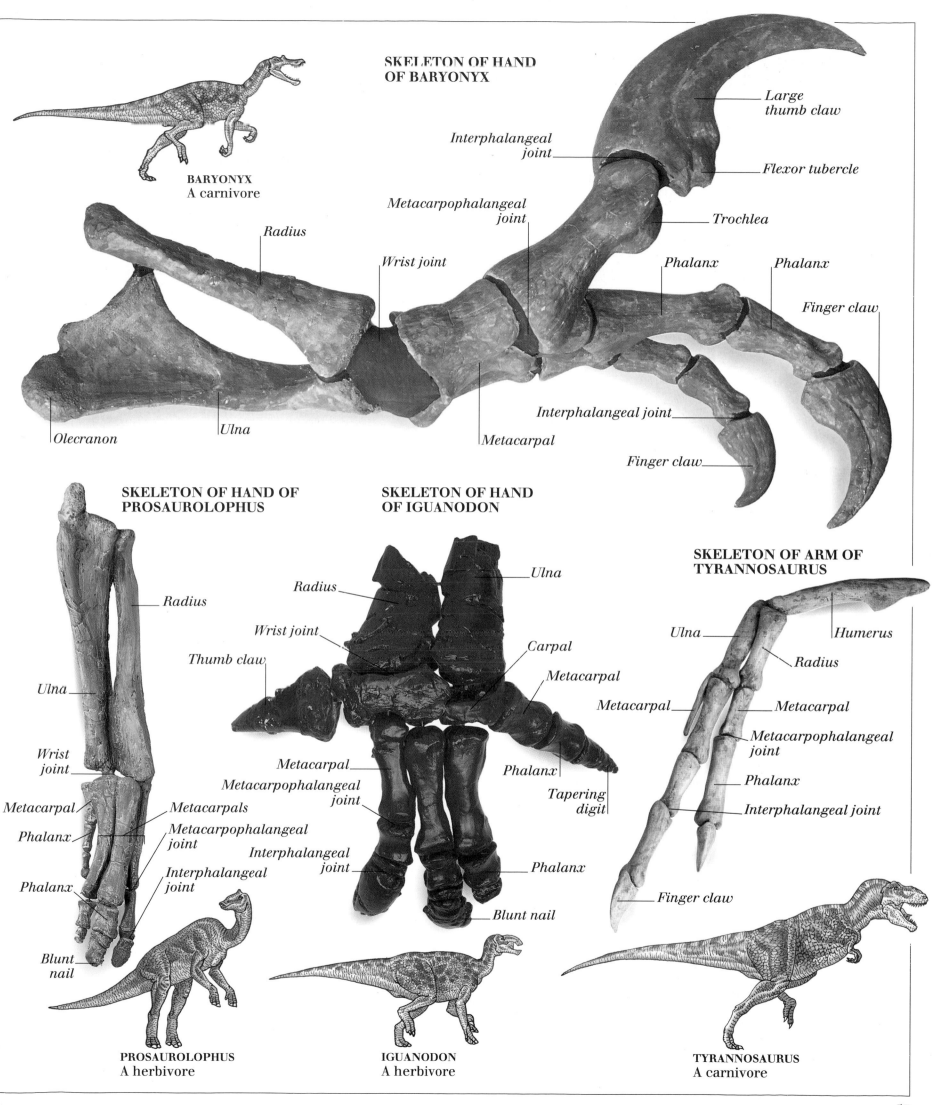

SKELETON OF HAND OF BARYONYX

BARYONYX
A carnivore

Large thumb claw

Interphalangeal joint

Flexor tubercle

Metacarpophalangeal joint

Trochlea

Radius

Wrist joint

Phalanx

Phalanx

Finger claw

Olecranon

Ulna

Interphalangeal joint

Metacarpal

Finger claw

SKELETON OF HAND OF PROSAUROLOPHUS

SKELETON OF HAND OF IGUANODON

SKELETON OF ARM OF TYRANNOSAURUS

Radius

Ulna

Radius

Wrist joint

Carpal

Ulna

Humerus

Thumb claw

Metacarpal

Radius

Ulna

Metacarpal

Metacarpal

Wrist joint

Metacarpal

Phalanx

Metacarpophalangeal joint

Metacarpal

Metacarpals

Metacarpophalangeal joint

Tapering digit

Phalanx

Phalanx

Metacarpophalangeal joint

Interphalangeal joint

Interphalangeal joint

Phalanx

Phalanx

Blunt nail

Finger claw

Blunt nail

PROSAUROLOPHUS
A herbivore

IGUANODON
A herbivore

TYRANNOSAURUS
A carnivore

Feet and tracks

SKELETON OF FOOT OF PLATEOSAURUS

DINOSAURS HAD HIGH ankles and walked on their toes. However, apart from these common characteristics, the feet of dinosaurs were extremely diverse. For example, *Stegosaurus*, a large, heavy dinosaur that walked on all fours (a quadruped), had broad, short, elephant-like feet. In contrast, certain large, heavy, semi-quadrupeds (quadrupedal dinosaurs that sometimes walked or ran on their hind legs), such as *Parasaurolophus* and *Iguanodon*, had longer feet with separate toes. Smaller, lighter dinosaurs that walked on two legs (bipeds), such as *Chirostenotes*, *Compsognathus*, and *Dromiceiomimus*, had relatively long, narrow, birdlike feet. The fossilized tracks of some dinosaurs indicate not only the structure of their feet, but also how they moved. For example, the tracks of *Ornithomimus* confirm that it was bipedal, and also indicate that it was lightweight and could run quickly.

Imprint of foot of Ornithomimus

Imprint of toe

Imprint of toe

Material of cast

FOOT OF STEGOSAURUS

FOOT OF COMPSOGNATHUS

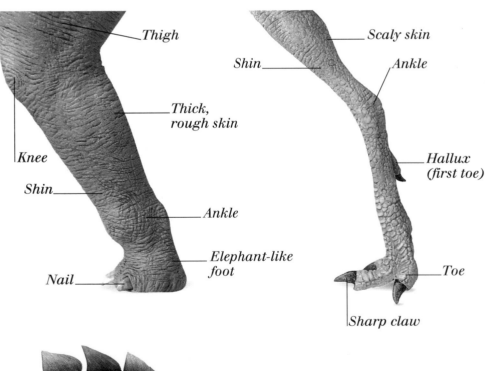

Thigh

Thick, rough skin

Knee

Shin

Ankle

Nail

Elephant-like foot

Scaly skin

Shin

Ankle

Hallux (first toe)

Toe

Sharp claw

CAST OF FOSSILIZED IGUANODON TRACK

Imprint of hindfoot of Iguanodon

Material of cast

Imprint of toe

STEGOSAURUS
Length: 30 ft (9.1 m)

COMPSOGNATHUS
Length: 28 in (70 cm)

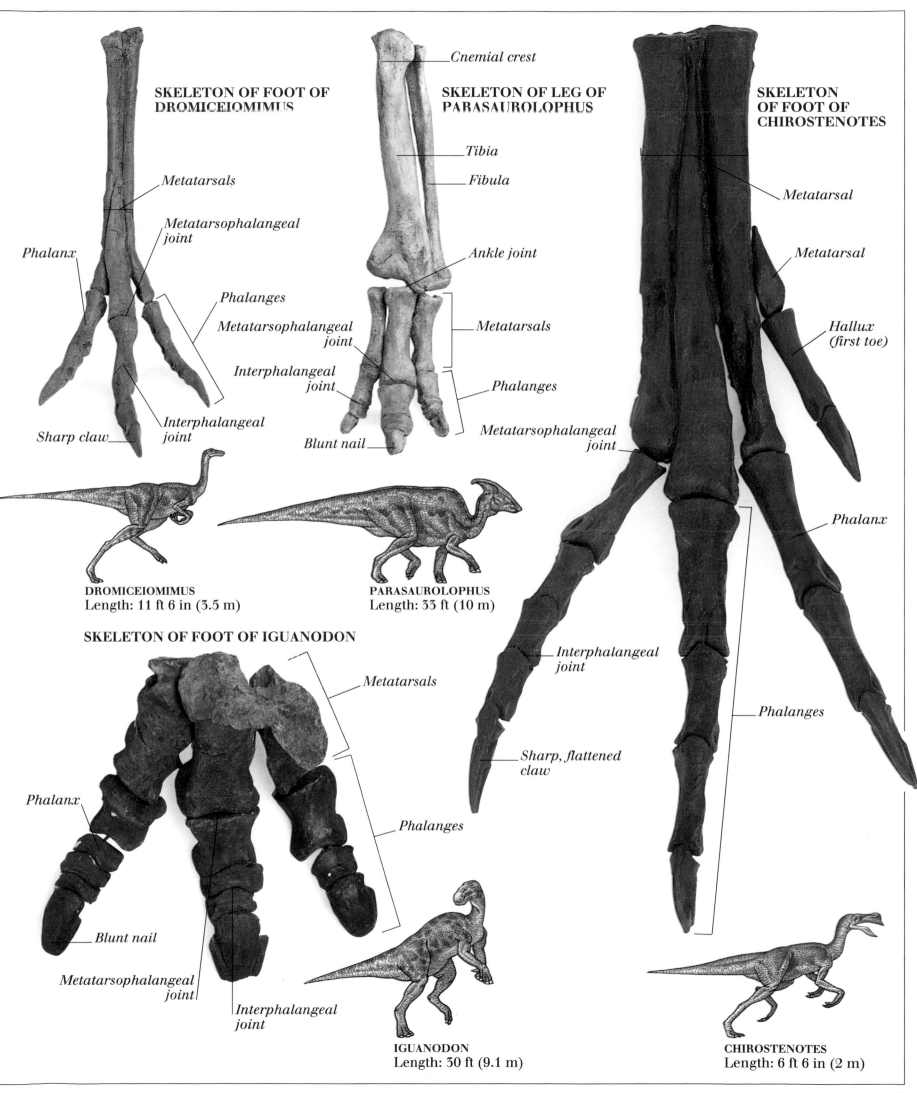

SKELETON OF FOOT OF DROMICEIOMIMUS

Metatarsals

Metatarsophalangeal joint

Phalanx

Phalanges

Metatarsophalangeal joint

Interphalangeal joint

Interphalangeal joint

Sharp claw

DROMICEIOMIMUS
Length: 11 ft 6 in (3.5 m)

SKELETON OF LEG OF PARASAUROLOPHUS

Cnemial crest

Tibia

Fibula

Ankle joint

Metatarsals

Metatarsophalangeal joint

Interphalangeal joint

Phalanges

Metatarsophalangeal joint

Blunt nail

PARASAUROLOPHUS
Length: 33 ft (10 m)

SKELETON OF FOOT OF CHIROSTENOTES

Metatarsal

Metatarsal

Hallux (first toe)

Phalanx

Metatarsophalangeal joint

Interphalangeal joint

Phalanges

Sharp, flattened claw

CHIROSTENOTES
Length: 6 ft 6 in (2 m)

SKELETON OF FOOT OF IGUANODON

Metatarsals

Phalanx

Phalanges

Blunt nail

Metatarsophalangeal joint

Interphalangeal joint

IGUANODON
Length: 30 ft (9.1 m)

Dinosaur relatives

MOST DINOSAURS BECAME EXTINCT about 65 million years ago. However, modern birds are considered to be living dinosaurs, while crocodiles are generally thought to be the dinosaurs' closest living relatives. It has been suggested that birds and dinosaurs diverged from a common ancestor during the Early Jurassic (208–188 million years ago). However, the most widely accepted view is that birds evolved from small, bipedal (two-legged) dinosaurs, such as *Deinonychus*. The principal evidence for this relationship is the similarity between the limb bones of *Coelophysis*, *Archaeopteryx* (the oldest known bird), and modern birds: all have forelimbs with three digits, and hindlimbs with four toes, one of which is a reversed hallux (first toe). Possibly descended from *Archaeopteryx* were *Ichthyornis* and *Hesperornis*, both birds of the Late Cretaceous (97.5–65 million years ago), and the more modern (but extinct) *Diatryma*, *Paleospheniscus*, and *Presbyornis*, as well as present-day birds. Crocodiles are only remotely related to the dinosaurs, because the two groups evolved along different lines after splitting off from a common ancestral group during the Early Triassic (248–243 million years ago).

FOSSIL OF A BIRD'S FEATHER

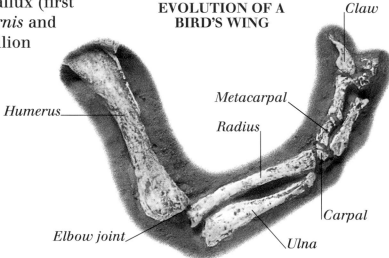

HESPERORNIS REGALIS
Length: 6 ft (1.8 m)

EVOLUTION OF A BIRD'S WING

Claw
Metacarpal
Radius
Humerus
Elbow joint
Carpal
Ulna

SKELETON OF FORELIMB OF COELOPHYSIS

EXTERNAL FEATURES OF ARCHAEOPTERYX

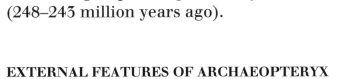

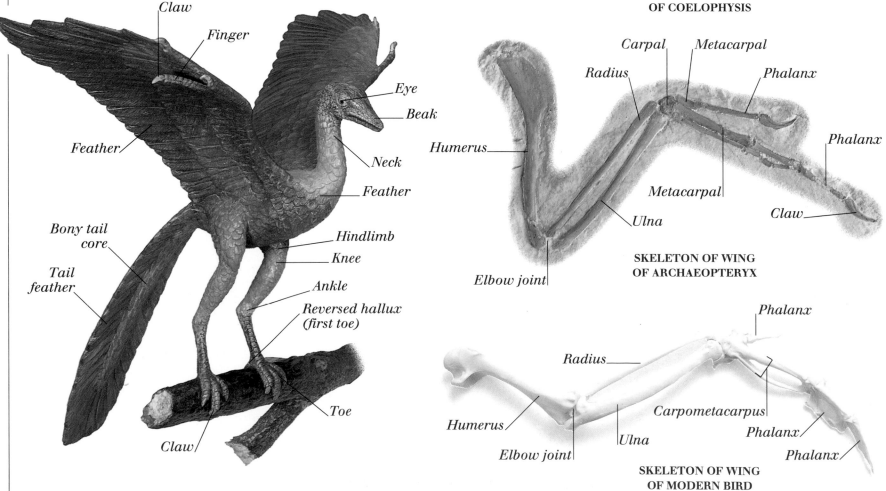

Claw
Finger
Eye
Beak
Neck
Feather
Feather
Hindlimb
Knee
Ankle
Reversed hallux (first toe)
Bony tail core
Tail feather
Toe
Claw

Carpal
Metacarpal
Radius
Phalanx
Humerus
Phalanx
Metacarpal
Ulna
Claw
Elbow joint

SKELETON OF WING OF ARCHAEOPTERYX

Phalanx
Radius
Humerus
Carpometacarpus
Elbow joint
Ulna
Phalanx
Phalanx

SKELETON OF WING OF MODERN BIRD

EXAMPLES OF EXTINCT BIRDS

PRESBYORNIS PERVETUS
Height: 3 ft 3 in (1 m)

PALEOSPHENISCUS PATAGONICUS
Height: 26 in (66 cm)

ICHTHYORNIS DISPAR
Length: 8 in (20 cm)

DIATRYMA GIGANTEA
Height: 7 ft (2.1 m)

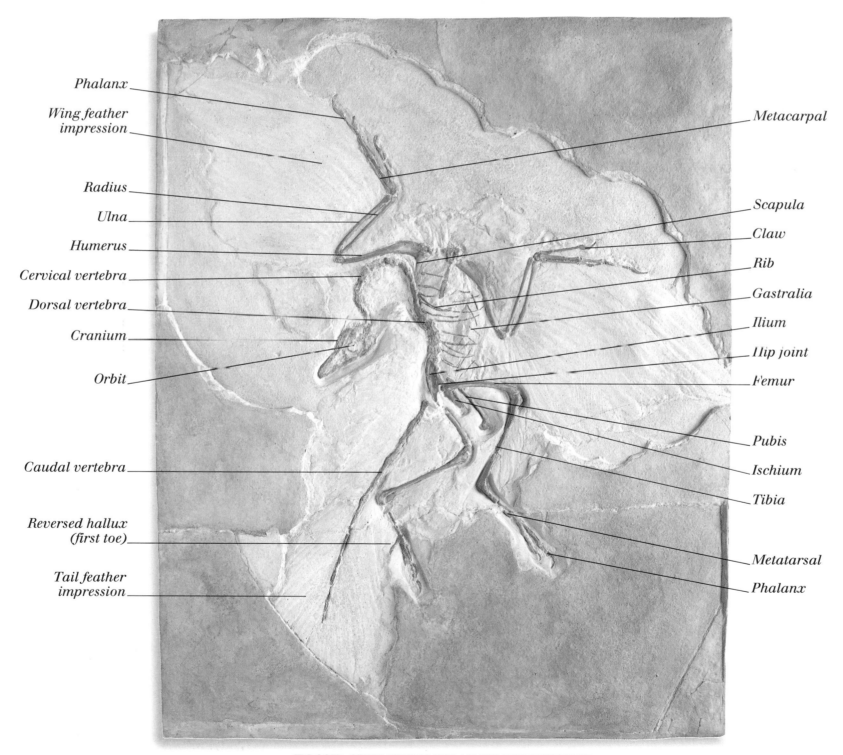

Phalanx

Wing feather impression

Radius

Ulna

Humerus

Cervical vertebra

Dorsal vertebra

Cranium

Orbit

Caudal vertebra

Reversed hallux (first toe)

Tail feather impression

Metacarpal

Scapula

Claw

Rib

Gastralia

Ilium

Hip joint

Femur

Pubis

Ischium

Tibia

Metatarsal

Phalanx

FOSSIL SKELETON OF ARCHAEOPTERYX

Dinosaur classification

THE CLASSIFICATION OF DINOSAURS is controversial and is continually
being revised in the light of new fossil finds and reinterpretations of
existing evidence. There are also a number of different methods of
classification. The method used here is based on inherited features
shared by members of a group but not by any members in other groups.
According to this classification, all dinosaurs and their relatives belong
to the major group Archosauria (ruling reptiles). The Archosauria can
be split into two main divisions: primitive archosaurs, which include
Proterosuchia, Erythrosuchia, *Euparkeria*, and Crurotarsi; and
ornithodiran archosaurs, which include Pterosauria, *Lagosuchus*, and
the Dinosauria. The Dinosauria ("true" dinosaurs) can be divided in
turn into three groups: Herrerasauria (early predatory dinosaurs),
Saurischia (lizard-hipped dinosaurs), and Ornithischia (bird-hipped
dinosaurs). Each group can then be subdivided down to the levels of
families (with names ending in "-idae"), genera (indicated by italics
in this chart), and species.

KEY

- ARCHOSAURS (RULING REPTILES)
- PRIMITIVE ARCHOSAURS
- ORNITHODIRAN ARCHOSAURS
- FLYING ARCHOSAURS
- DINOSAUR-LIKE ARCHOSAURS
- DINOSAURS
- EARLY PREDATORY DINOSAURS
- LIZARD-HIPPED DINOSAURS
- BIRD-HIPPED DINOSAURS

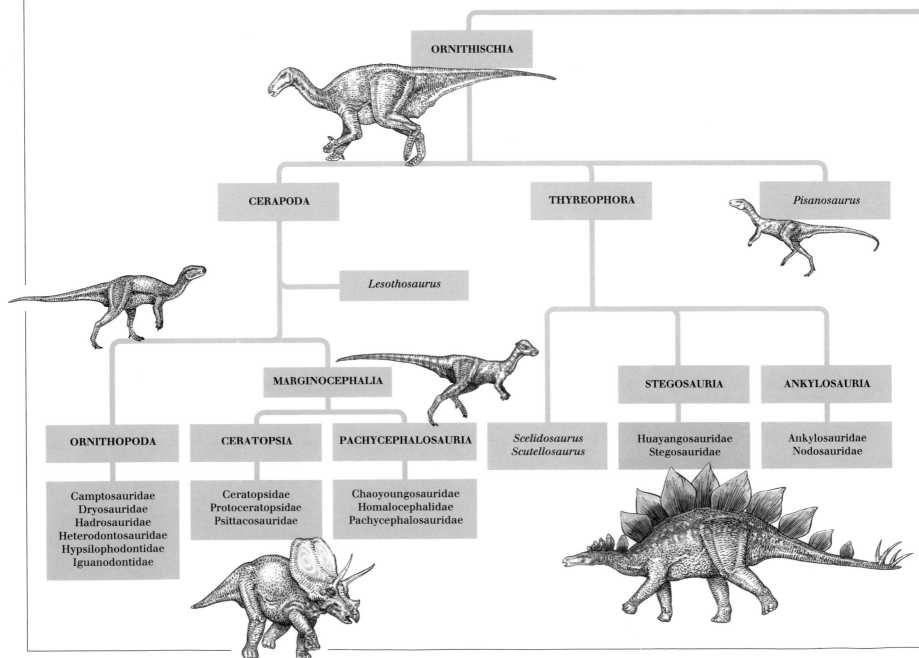

ORNITHISCHIA

CERAPODA   THYREOPHORA   *Pisanosaurus*

Lesothosaurus

MARGINOCEPHALIA   STEGOSAURIA   ANKYLOSAURIA

ORNITHOPODA   CERATOPSIA   PACHYCEPHALOSAURIA   *Scelidosaurus* *Scutellosaurus*   Huayangosauridae Stegosauridae   Ankylosauridae Nodosauridae

Camptosauridae
Dryosauridae
Hadrosauridae
Heterodontosauridae
Hypsilophodontidae
Iguanodontidae

Ceratopsidae
Protoceratopsidae
Psittacosauridae

Chaoyoungosauridae
Homalocephalidae
Pachycephalosauridae

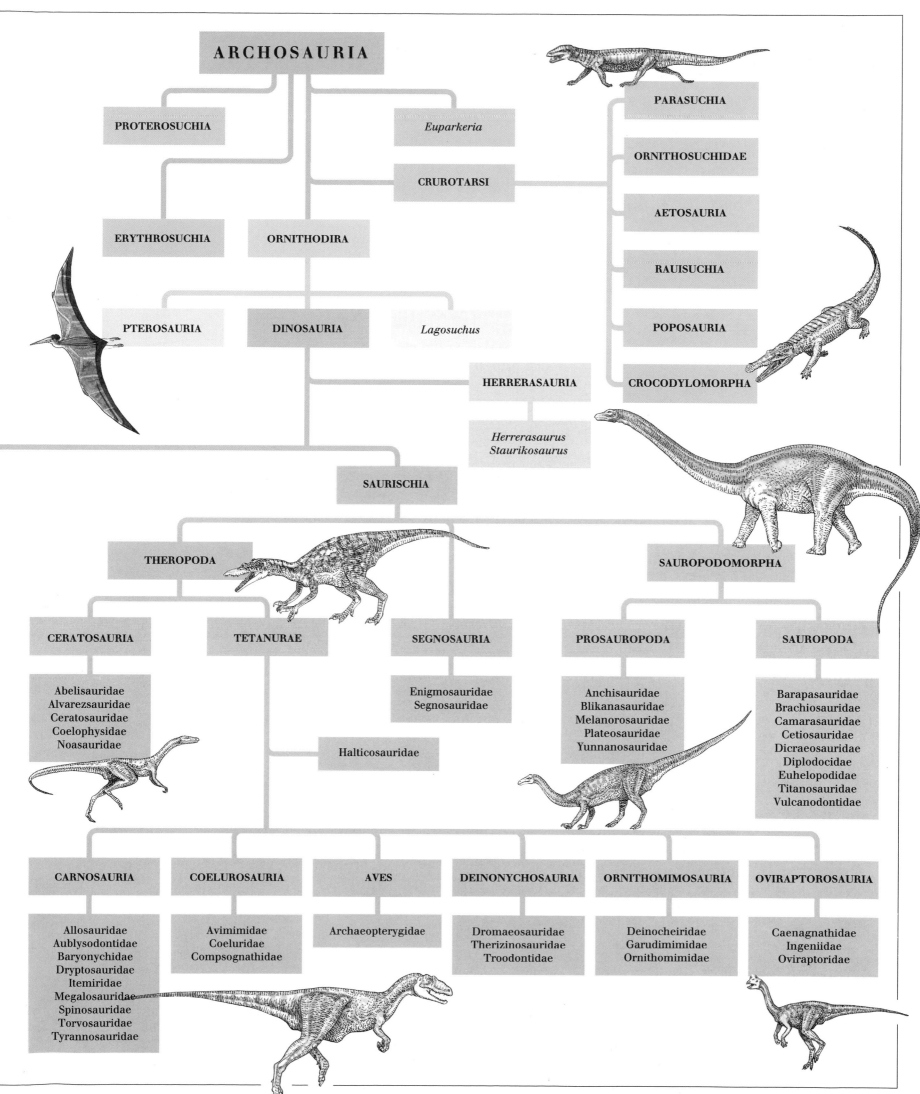

ARCHOSAURIA

PROTEROSUCHIA

Euparkeria

CRUROTARSI

PARASUCHIA

ORNITHOSUCHIDAE

AETOSAURIA

RAUISUCHIA

POPOSAURIA

CROCODYLOMORPHA

ERYTHROSUCHIA

ORNITHODIRA

PTEROSAURIA

DINOSAURIA

Lagosuchus

HERRERASAURIA

Herrerasaurus
Staurikosaurus

SAURISCHIA

THEROPODA

SAUROPODOMORPHA

CERATOSAURIA

Abelisauridae
Alvarezsauridae
Ceratosauridae
Coelophysidae
Noasauridae

TETANURAE

Halticosauridae

SEGNOSAURIA

Enigmosauridae
Segnosauridae

PROSAUROPODA

Anchisauridae
Blikanasauridae
Melanorosauridae
Plateosauridae
Yunnanosauridae

SAUROPODA

Barapasauridae
Brachiosauridae
Camarasauridae
Cetiosauridae
Dicraeosauridae
Diplodocidae
Euhelopodidae
Titanosauridae
Vulcanodontidae

CARNOSAURIA

Allosauridae
Aublysodontidae
Baryonychidae
Dryptosauridae
Itemiridae
Megalosauridae
Spinosauridae
Torvosauridae
Tyrannosauridae

COELUROSAURIA

Avimimidae
Coeluridae
Compsognathidae

AVES

Archaeopterygidae

DEINONYCHOSAURIA

Dromaeosauridae
Therizinosauridae
Troodontidae

ORNITHOMIMOSAURIA

Deinocheiridae
Garudimimidae
Ornithomimidae

OVIRAPTOROSAURIA

Caenagnathidae
Ingeniidae
Oviraptoridae

Index

Acknowledgments

Dorling Kindersley would like to thank:
Dr. Monty Reid, Andrew Neuman, and the staff at the Royal Tyrrell Museum of Palaeontology, Drumheller, Alberta; Dr. Angela Milner and the staff at the Department of Palaeontology, the Natural History Museum, London; Professor W. Ziegler and the staff, in particular Michael Loderstaedt, at the Naturmuseum Senckenburg, Frankfurt; Dr. Alexander Liebau, Axel Hunghrebüller, Reiner Schoch, and the staff at the Institut und Museum für Geologie und Paläontologie der Universität, Tübingen; Rupert Wild at the Institut für Paläontologie, Staatliches Museum für Naturkunde, Stuttgart; Dr. Scheiber, the Stadtmuseum, Nördlingen; Professor Dr. Dietrich Herm, Staatssammlung für Paläontologie und Historische Geologie, München; Dr. Michael Keith-Lucas, Department of Botany, University of Reading; Dr. Richard Walker. For skeletons: the Royal Tyrrell Museum of Palaeontology, Alberta: *Dromaeosaurus* pp. 16-17, *Gryposaurus* pp. 38-39, *Heterodontosaurus* p. 35, *Maiasaura* p. 38, *Ornitholestes* p. 15, *Ornithomimus* pp. 18-19, *Parasaurolophus* pp. 40-41, *Stegoceras* pp. 46-47,

Struthiomimus p. 19, *Triceratops* pp. 50-51; Naturmuseum Senckenberg, Frankfurt: *Archaeopteryx* p. 57, *Diplodocus* pp. 28-29, *Iguanodon* p. 36, *Tyrannosaurus* pp. 22-23, *Stegosaurus* p. 43; Institut und Museum für Geologie und Paläontologie der Universität Tübingen: *Plateosaurus* pp. 24-25, *Kentrosaurus* p. 43; the Natural History Museum, London: *Baryonyx* p. 21, *Tuojiangosaurus* p. 43; Staatliches Museum für Naturkunde, Stuttgart: *Coelophysis* p. 15, *Compsognathus* p. 14; American Museum of Natural History, New York: *Protoceratops* pp. 48-49

Model makers:
John Holmes: *Euoplocephalus* pp. 44-45, *Gallimimus* pp. 18-19, *Hypsilophodon* pp. 34-35; Roby Braun: *Anchisaurus* pp. 24-25, *Compsognathus* pp. 14-15, *Stegosaurus* pp. 42-43; Centaur Studios: *Barosaurus* pp. 28-29, *Baryonyx* pp. 20-21, *Brachiosaurus* pp. 26-27, *Corythosaurus* pp. 40-41, *Iguanodon* pp. 36-37, *Triceratops* p. 50; David Donkin: Cretaceous globe p. 13, Jurassic globe p. 11, Triassic globe p. 9

Additional consultancy:
William Lindsay; Lowell Dingus (American Museum of Natural History, New York)

Additional photography:
John Downs, Tim Parmenter, and Colin Keates (Natural History Museum, London); Lynton Gardiner (American Museum of Natural History, New York); Steve Gorton; Dave King

Photographic assistance:
Kevin Zak; Gary Ombler

Additional design assistance:
Lesley Betts; Christina Betts

Additional editorial assistance:
Jacqui Hand; Jeanette Cossar

Index:
Kay Wright